T0338073

Statistical Process Control for the Food Industry

Statistical Process Control for the Food Industry

A Guide for Practitioners and Managers

Sarina Abdul Halim Lim
Department of Food Technology
Faculty of Food Science and Technology
Universiti Putra Malaysia
Malaysia

Jiju Antony
Director of Process Improvement
Department of Business Management
School of Social Sciences
Heriot-Watt University
UK

Registered Offices
John Wiley & Sons, Inc., 111 River Street, Hoboken, NJ 07030, USA
John Wiley & Sons Ltd, The Atrium, Southern Gate, Chichester, West Sussex, PO19 8SQ, UK

Editorial Office
9600 Garsington Road, Oxford, OX4 2DQ, UK

For details of our global editorial offices, customer services, and more information about Wiley products visit us at www.wiley.com.

Library of Congress Cataloging-in-Publication Data applied for

ISBN: 9781119151982

Cover Design: Wiley
Cover Image: © IriGri/Shutterstock

Set in 10/12pt WarnockPro by SPi Global, Chennai, India

Printed in Great Britain by TJ International Ltd, Padstow, Cornwall.

10 9 8 7 6 5 4 3 2 1

Contents

Preface

Quality and process control are two important fields in the area of food quality management and currently the improvement of both areas being used as a strategic approach to surviving in the competitive but highly regulated industry. Food quality control is the subject of attention in the food production lines. This book refers to quality control, not in the constricted meaning of the term that is often used within the industry where there are hazards such as microbial, chemical and physical assessment of the product. The authors offer the readers the opportunity to view quality control as the reactive activity that involves controllable factors, which affect the quality of the finished product. The most reliable and renowned technique to address process control in the realm of quality management is one based on the statistical method. Unlike other statistical quality control manuals, this book does not cover the heavy topic of the manual calculation on developing control charts. Instead, it covers the process in implementing SPC such as readiness, planning, and managing the SPC implementation. In adopting the technique, it is critical for the managers to understand 'what, where, who, when and how'. It was therefore deemed preferable to include discussion on the related issues on SPC implementation in the industry, such as challenges, advantageous of the implementation and the relation of SPC application towards process performance. Another critical area that is often being missed in the industry is the preparedness of business to deploy SPC implementation. A self-assessment tool is provided for the managers to assess their business preparedness level before investing in the SPC application. The book also covers another significant phase of SPC implementation, which is the 'implementation phase'. Managers and practitioners can benefit from a step-by-step cookbook approach on the SPC implementation provided in this book.

This book is divided into 10 chapters. Part 1 covers the philosophy and fundamentals of quality control in the food industry. Chapter 1: Introduction to the food quality management, the role of SPC in quality management, the importance of SPC in the food industry. Chapter 2 briefs the readers on the food industry chain. Chapter 3 introduces the readers the nomenclature of quality and the interlink of quality and food safety. Chapter 4 introduces the application of SPC and its role in the food industry. Chapter 5 covers the basic tools of SPC and how these tools work in the food manufacturing context. Part 2 covers the stages involve in implementing SPC in the food businesses. Chapter 6 illustrates the importance of team formation for implementing and sustaining an SPC initiative in the organisational setting, the roles and responsibilities of team members will be clearly addressed. Chapter 7 elucidates the readiness factors and a self-assessment tool for the implementation of SPC in the food industry. Chapter 8 presents the critical element in implementing SPC such as critical success factors, challenges, benefits and process performance measurement. Chapter 9 provides a systematic and disciplined set of guidelines showing how to get started with an SPC initiative as well as how to deploy it company-wide. Chapter 10 presents case studies of SPC application in the food industry on both the quality and safety aspect. This book may serve as a cookbook for the managers in the food industry to assess their readiness to adopt SPC in the company and initiating the SPC application in their respective companies.

1

Quality Management in the Food Industry

1.1 Introduction

The importance of quality in the food industry has grown significantly over recent decades as consumers have become more critical. Apart from that, this is also attributed to the increasing expectations of consumers, stricter governmental regulations, changes in consumption patterns, continuous development of technologies and expanding market competition. Compared to other industry, food quality management is challenging due to the complex character of food products with the unpredictable and evolving behaviour of people involved in the food chain. Therefore, food companies are seeking more efficient and effective managerial approaches to improve or sustain the quality aspect of their processes and products. The key forces that drive the food companies to seek quality management practices may be dictated by internal or external circumstances or maybe both. The key purpose of effective quality management is to boost the competitiveness of the business and offer strategic advantages in the market (Anderson, Rungtusanatham, and Schroeder 1994). Similarly, food quality management is crucial to assure the quality of the process and subsequently the products in food businesses.

> *Although the food industry is aware of the negative public opinion, not all companies are committed to improving the industry's image*
> Mike Doyle, PhD, Director of the Center for Food Safety

1.2 Definition of Quality Control

The term 'quality control' (QC) is initiated from the field of engineering where the quality of the product is constructing the quality of the product instead of inspecting the quality. Scoping down to the core of quality control, it is understood as a procedure designed to ensure that the product conforms to a designated set of criteria as set out by the consumers.

Statistical Process Control for the Food Industry: A Guide for Practitioners and Managers, First Edition.
Sarina Abdul Halim Lim and Jiju Antony.

Quality control has been prioritised after the World War II where mass production manufacturing was developed despite the fact that quality is always being integrated into the businesses since the industrial revolution in Europe. Therefore, the quality control activities took a significant turn where the demand for more inspectors in ensuring the quality of the product increased. Another major advancement of quality control is when a physician, Dr. Walter Shewhart introduced a statistical approach to quality control in 1924. It started after World War II, when Statistical Quality Control has been widely applied to assist in quality control and production.

The key objectives of quality control are:

• to achieve a consistent quality of the product;
• to maintain the product at the quality at levels and tolerance limits acceptable to the consumers while minimising the cost for the vendors;
• to manage and continuously sustain the expected level of the product quality; and
• to ensure that produced items are fulfilling the highest possible quality.

Quality control can be categorised as off-line quality control and on-line quality control. The key purpose of the quality control is to satisfy the standard of quality in the product being produced as is compatible with the market for which the product is designed and at a price the product will be sold. Thus, the best approach of quality control is to initiate the efforts in the product design phase and continuously apply such efforts through the production operation phases.

1.3 Quality Control in the Food Industry

In modern food manufacturing settings, the quality control systems are the supporting programs that are outcrops of the Hazard Analysis Critical Control Point (HACCP) program. A clear indication of the product conformance to their specification are based in the documentation required in the HACCP program.

Typically, any quality control program in this industry is documented in the program general overview and being verified on a monitoring form. The data gained through documentation, observation, measurement, data analysis and documentation from the programs provided a clear picture of the product conformance to a specification. The common approach to document the overall control system, a form for the quality control scheme should be completed. Thus, this document provided a concise indication of all the quality related programs established by the company (e.g. quality parameters, the specification limits, sampling plan, action plan, critical control point (CCP), and correction action).

Quality control of food refers scientifically to the utilisation of technological, physical, chemical, microbiological, nutritional, and sensory parameters to achieve wholesome food. These quality factors depend on specific attributes, such as sensory properties (e.g. flavour, colour, aroma, taste, texture), quantitative properties (e.g. percentage of sugar, protein, fibre) and hidden attributes (e.g. peroxides, free fatty acids, and enzyme) (Edith and Ochubiojo 2012). Quality control is commonly in the raw material, process control, and finished product in the food industry.

Most large food businesses establish a quality control department in the organisation as they have a crucial role in driving quality efforts. A team of Quality Control (QC) staff promotes quality in the department, assists, and closely consults with the production. Typically, the production department is directly responsible for the quality of the products. Nevertheless, unlike most people's perception, quality assurance (QA) is not directly responsible for the quality of the products the business delivered to its customers. The professionals of the QC department:

- assist the production in quality-related matters;
- report to the division director of QA;
- seek direction and assistance from the vice president of QA; and
- support for QA programs.

1.3.1 Quality Control (Raw Material)

In producing the products, the food manufacturers have to purchase other products in different forms and services to ensure the business maintains production. The products in the food industry are enormously diverse including raw materials from processed food ingredients, minor and major ingredients in food production.

In the chain of food production, especially in handling the production of the consumer foods, it requires the manufacturers who purchase the ingredients, raw materials and food packaging to ensure the materials are safe and fit for use. Apart from that, the food manufacturers have to identify the impact of supplies and services purchased on quality and subsequently confirm the supplier's capability to meet the requirements of the specification. Thus, many food companies categorised the quality control of these ingredients as being under supplier and purchasing control. Despite purchasing services are not as important as many of the ingredients, services such as pest control, calibration, laundry, plant cleaning and quality consultancy need to be considered. Therefore, the disruption of the food production commonly stemming from the supplier problems may impact the production, customers and the business bottom-line. Food companies should have a systematic control plan in place. Such a systematic control plan is the key focus of the quality management system (QMS) in a company which prevents problems and ensures consistency within the manufacturing process.

Typically, the supplier provides the raw materials, which means the quality of the raw materials is not under the direct control of the manufacturer. Nevertheless, the manufacturers can overcome this through their purchasing power where the manufacturers have significant opportunity to select suppliers. The company takes the initiative to have a clear understanding of what is required. Thus, these demands have to be translated into criteria for selecting the suppliers and requirements for them to fulfil.

According to the ISO9001 requirement on the suppliers (i.e. external provider), the companies are only required to define the process, identify the authorised people, and ensure that the practice is implemented and adequately controlled. Nevertheless, the organisation needs to develop and establish procedures that work efficiently for them.

1.3.2 Quality Control in Production (Processes and End Product)

The actual processing approaches are critical in-house factors that may adversely affect quality. The most common process control involved in the food manufacturing process is in the area of the production process despite some operators using the term 'production' and 'processing' interchangeably. The quality programmes in food industry increase the awareness relating to the values of quality of production and production control strategy as their fundamental elements. Quality control activities in the food industry mainly emphasise the production area of the business function.

Controls in production processes are critical in the food businesses as process variation contributes to the total variation of production. Such principles necessitate producer strategies in the manufacturing process in such a manner that the process can be run in controlled conditions at all steps of the food production. Furthermore, such an element of process control in a food quality programme is identified as being critical for the excellent capability of the process and consistent quality of the products. The food manufacturer should plan a process control scheme. Thus, in this book, we have specifically guided the manufacturers in implementing process control through the statistical approach in Chapter 9. The common process control scheme planning should include process mapping, identification of critical points, a monitoring plan and correction plan. It is very efficient to list the sequence of the steps in the process such as in process map or flowchart approach in controlling the process (Figure 1.1).

Based on the process map in the example above, there are several important critical areas which require sampling and 'checkpoint' for quality control activities. A process is a collection of mutually related resources and activities,

Figure 1.1 Example of process map of bread production.

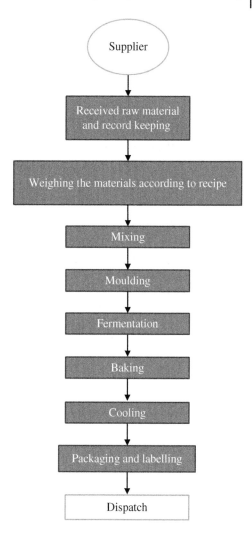

which transforms input into output. Process control covers all activities from the conversion of customers' demands into manufacturing instructions through the production and subsequently to the packaging, delivery, and sales of the products. Thus, in the industry, the use of process control can be regarded as a bigger or smaller extent of the operation management.

In this book, quality control of the process refers at the production process of the food and also covers in any activities that involved processes associated towards the quality of the product and services in the food industry. The inspection of the finished product is considered as the main approach for quality control in the conventional quality control of the processes. The example of service processes in the food industry are:

- handling customer complaints;
- the time needed to handle customer demand;
- human resource;
- erroneous billing; and
- time for certification.

Inevitably, the success of any food manufacturing operation is highly based on the degree of control exerted on the different steps in the food production.

1.3.3 Issues Related to the Quality Control

1.3.3.1 Late Adopters

The food industry mainly comprises of small and medium-sized companies, which results in the late adoption of quality management approaches in the industry. The industry has lagged behind and suffered a severe food quality crisis despite the food industry being the pioneer in the field of quality assurance and quality management. The lack of priority in updating quality management approaches may also cause the industry quality management practices to fall behind other industries. The principal occurrences of the food crises arise from the vague responsibilities for food safety, where it is arbitrarily divided between government, public authorities, private businesses and politicians.

1.3.3.2 Difficulties Identifying and Prioritising Hazards (Microbiological and Chemical)

In the food industry, there are many points that could contribute towards the food quality and food safety attribute. Nevertheless, it is financially impossible to implement a quality control assessment at all points in the real practice. Therefore, it is highly suggested to implement the prioritisation of the control point to provide the food company with a correct direction of their quality control strategy (i.e. by monitoring and controlling the most critical points towards food safety and quality of the food production). Identification of critical points is commonly conducted based on experiences of the staff. The manual or guidelines for the certification process (e.g. HACCP) often provide approaches to identify these critical points.

1.3.3.3 Lack of Scientific and Quantitative Method to Assess Critical Points

The critical points in the food processes may or may not have direct measurement parameters. The root of the problem has been identified as:

- lack of scientific data;
- different approaches to monitoring the critical points;
- variation in standards resulting in different assessments on safety; and
- lack of awareness on the systematic control technique.

1.4 Quality Assurance

Generally, the quality system can be defined as the organisational structure, responsibilities, processes, procedures, and resources that facilitate the achievement of quality management. On the other hand, the organisational structure is the formal form of functions and tasks and the connection between them and the order of the processes within the organisation (Ren, He, and Luning 2016). QA systems only cover different aspects of the complete quality system in an organisation.

Over the last few years, the outcome of food crises has been a dramatically increased awareness by consumers and has alerted government bodies on food safety issues. The implementation of the control system under the food safety system has become an emerging issue for all stakeholders in the sector. QA standards and guidelines are increasingly implemented by many food organisations to regain consumer trust in food quality and safety and to establish their company-specific food safety management system.

If quality is the key goal of a food company, the director of quality assurance commonly holds a top management position, and quality matters should be reported directly to the president of the company. Food production systems have to be controlled by technological and managerial measures by applying QA (Ren, He, and Luning 2016).

Moreover, QA outlines and manages the activities of control, audits, evaluation, and regulatory aspects of a food production system. For instance, it covers an in-house consulting organisation, evaluates the quality program and offers advice, suggestions, and instructions for safety and quality improvement. Apart from that, instead of blaming culture practices which occur in some companies through the QA, QA does in fact, have the advisory function in the QMS of a company.

In a food QMS, a number of common quality assurance systems (QASs) are available such as:

- Current Good Manufacturing Practice (cGMP)
- Good Hygiene Practice (GHP)
- Hazard Analysis Critical Control Points (HACCP)
- International Organisation for Standardisation (ISO)
- British Retail Consortium (BRC)
- Food Safety System Certification 22000 (FSSC22000)

1.4.1 Current Good Manufacturing Practice (cGMP)

Good manufacturing practice (GMP) has a legal status in the USA where it is codified in the Food and Drug Administration (FDA) cGMP Regulations for foods (which cover all foods and specific regulations for specific food categories).

This certification is highly concerned with the hygiene requirements for food producers to supply safe food. Nevertheless, there is no absolute assurance of food safety as hazards abound to exist at each food process. The key target is to ensure the absence of unacceptable risks of the processes and environment in manufacturing the products, or a few academics borrow the term from the World Trade Organisation, 'An Appropriate Level of Protection' (ALOP). Various criteria are used as the basis for GMP complement assessment which includes personal hygiene, food production facilities sanitation and design, process control and pest control.

The fundamentals of GMP for food are:

- *Quality control.* Product meets specifications.
- *Quality assurance.* Systems ensure control and consistency.
- *Documentation.* If it is not documented, it did not happen, or it is a false alarm.
- Verification and self-inspection.

> HACCP augments and refines codes of Good Manufacturing Practices in that it concentrates effort and priorities for control on those requirements that are essential for safety.
>
> Baird-Parker and Mayes (1989)

The term 'good manufacturing practice' is not defined, despite it being used widely around the world. and it is assumed to consist of the sum total of the stated regulatory requirements, policy, procedures, and guidelines for complying with the food regulations. The FDA has announced the plan and processes involved in modernising the GMP for food safety (last revised in 1986).

The five important factors of production and food processes that affect quality and safety while following GMPs, are as follows:-

- *Place.* Premises should be clean, and equipment should be orderly arranged. Food preparation surfaces should allow for regular cleaning and should be designed to prevent food contamination.
- *Primary materials.* Materials should be assessed, controlled, tested, and recorded where the contaminated, adulterated, impure raw materials should be rejected and returned.
- *People.* Number of personnel must be in sufficient numbers, equipped with sufficient knowledge and training, qualified by education, and mature with experience to perform their respective tasks.
- *Process.* The sanitation plan should include procedures for effective premise cleaning, equipment, handling the health and hygienic behaviour of personnel.
- *Product.* Every product has its own specifications, which may include quantity, purity, potency and test methods.

1.4.2 HACCP (Hazard Analysis of Critical Control Point)

The application of HACCP to food manufacture was pioneered in the 1960s by the Pillsbury Company in conjunction with the United States Army Natick

Laboratory and NASA, the National Aeronautics and Space Administration to manufacture safe food for the astronauts. In the early 1970s, a considerable number of HACCP applications extended to the food industry.

The HACCP system is currently adopted by food companies worldwide as it is a logical, structured and scientific system that can monitor, control, and verify safety problems in food production. It involves a prevention process by which the hazards and risks associated with the manufacture, storage, and distribution of foods are identified and assessed and appropriate controls of CCPs, which either eliminate or reduce the hazards, are implemented at specific points.

1.4.3 ISO

ISO 22000 is one of the most renowned and well-established QMSs in the food sector. It is a system that focuses on food safety management suggesting the critical requirements for all food producers. Apart from that, it also involves the ability of companies to control hazards in terms of food safety, to conform to the regulatory requirements and to communicate food safety issues to all involved stakeholders. Thus, the implementation of the system makes the customer have confidence in the products.

1.4.4 British Retail Consortium

In the similar light, BRC standards were developed for food safety by the BRC. BRC standards are widely used, and it was used as the benchmark for best practice in the food industry. The standard response to the industry needs to provide the quality and operational criteria for suppliers, manufacturers, and global retailers to ensure compliance with legal and statutory requirements. The core requirements of this standard are the implementation of HACCP, documenting the quality management practices, processes, and personnel, and control of plant environment. Indicative examples of BRC standards include issues for food safety, consumer products, packaging and materials, storage and distribution, and best practice guidelines.

The nature of the QA system in the food industry may differ in several aspects where the system is developed by combining or integrating the aspects to ensure the food quality. There is no standard formulation on which the QAS should be integrated into a food business as each product, commodity, and company have different priorities.

1.5 Quality Management System in the Food Industry

QMS consists of the activities and decisions performed in an organisation to produce and maintain a product with the desired quality level against minimal costs (Luning and Marcelis 2009). QMS is highly related to the formalising of quality assurance policies, strategy, standards and specifications from a documented QAS (Early 2012). Moreover, QMS is a comprehensive approach to the quality assurance program in the food industry. The implementation of QMS is considered as the development of a food QAS that is heading to more systematic and structured quality assurance.

The 'food quality management' refers to dealing with the food safety and quality, food regulations, and quality management issues, which concerns with the system in production and also with the system of people. The system thinking hierarchy developed by food quality management (belongs to the higher system level) is known to be a complex system but assumed to be a controllable process. The food industry quality system introduces and uses a straightforward mechanism of control to manage the variation. It is represented by the great emphasis on the implementation of the QM (Quality Management) which are commonly based on the control circle to assure the food quality.

In the food industry, certification or third-party control has come to the fore as one of the quality management approaches. Food companies are entitled to use the certificate awarded to them in their marketing strategy. Therefore, the applicants (companies) are accredited or inspected for the main characteristics of certification systems by the independent bodies grounded on standards laid down by different external organisations (standard owners) of the key characteristics of the certifications. The figure below indicated the three main certifications in the food industry and highlighted the amount of statistical process control (SPC) usage (Figure 1.2).

1.6   Statistical Thinking

Various tools for quality improvement under the quality management belong to the application of statistical methods and the philosophy of statistical thinking. The process of adapting the fundamental change in the business in terms of economic, political, technological, and social character is connected to the quality management and the demand on the management of the modern organisation.

Snee (1990) stated that the principle of statistical thinking is:

- All works occur in a system of interconnected process;
- Variation exists in all processes; and
- Understanding and reducing variation are keys to success.

Based on the principle of statistical thinking, it is clear that statistical thinking is process-oriented thinking which provides a fundamental philosophical framework for quality improvement activities. Such activities focus on the processes, and identify and reduce the variation and the application of relevant data to understand the trend of the variation Cox and Efron (2017).

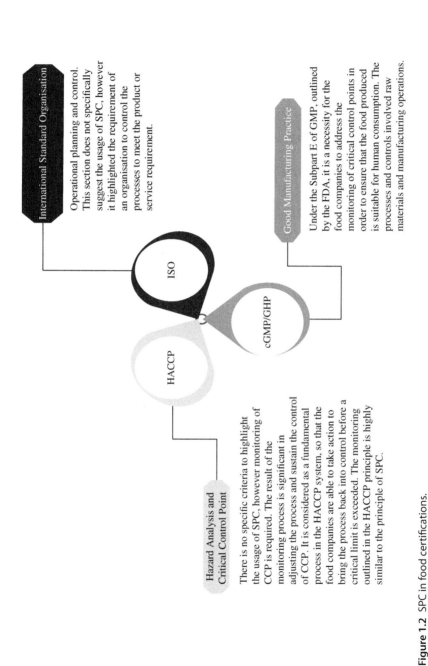

International Standard Organisation

Operational planning and control. This section does not specifically suggest the usage of SPC, however it highlighted the requirement of an organisation to control the processes to meet the product or service requirement.

ISO

Good Manufacturing Practice

Under the Subpart E of GMP, outlined by the FDA, it is a necessity for the food companies to address the monitoring of critical control points in order to ensure that the food produced is suitable for human consumption. The processes and controls involved raw materials and manufacturing operations.

cGMP/GHP

HACCP

Hazard Analysis and Critical Control Point

There is no specific criteria to highlight the usage of SPC, however monitoring of CCP is required. The result of the monitoring process is significant in adjusting the process and sustain the control of CCP. It is considered as a fundamental process in the HACCP system, so that the food companies are able to take action to bring the process back into control before a critical limit is exceeded. The monitoring outlined in the HACCP principle is highly similar to the principle of SPC.

Figure 1.2 SPC in food certifications.

1.7 Summary

- Quality in the food industry is considered as the most important aspect of the processes and production, and food safety is considered the most crucial aspect of the food quality.
- Quality control in the food industry is used to satisfy the standard of product quality and comply with the regulations and rules in ensuring the food is safe to be consumed.
- Quality control in the food industry is typically being implemented at raw material inspection, processes, and end product.
- The businesses in the food industry are lagging behind in adopting techniques in quality control and suffered a food quality crisis.
- Quality control involves inspection, monitoring, testing, measurement, and analysis of data.
- Quality assurance activities involve planning, audit projects and analysis of the quality programme.
- QMS refers to a formalised internal system that records the processes, procedures, and responsibilities for conforming to quality policies and objectives.
- QMS includes quality strategy, quality planning, and improvement activities in the business.

2

Food Industry and its Contribution to the Global Economy

2.1 Introduction

This chapter will provide an overview of the food industry and begins to bring the reasons behind Statistical Process Control (SPC) implementation in the industry. Food industry is a complex multitiered system of producers and consumers, which regulated by the state of agriculture, Ministry of Health and other governmental bodies that establish many regulations. In addition to the numerous law and regulations, today low margins, globalisation, decrease-trained employees' number and changing consumer distribution pattern also challenge food businesses to operate efficiently (Kennedy, Nantel, and Shetty 2004).

In the United Kingdom (UK), the food and beverage industry employ more than 100 000 workers, which is nearly a third of the European Union workforce (Malone 2017). The food and beverage industry contributed more than 28 billion GBP to the economy, and exports more than 20 billion GBP worth of food and drinks to the rest of the world last year (Malone 2017).

Interestingly, more than 96% of the businesses in the food and beverage industry in the UK are made out of SMEs, making it a competitive industry (Malone 2017). On the other hand, according to the Unnevehr (2017), the food and beverage industry accounts for at least 5% of the total gross domestic product in the United States. The food industry also contributes at least 10% of the employment rate, and more than 10% of consumers' disposable incomes in the United States. The food industry also recorded a high number of sales at USD 1.4 trillion dollars (Unnevehr 2017). The food industry is a major contributor in providing job opportunities in the food processing, manufacturing, distribution, and sales of food.

The food industry has also been reported to be more reliable compared to other industries within the manufacturing industry. It helps to contribute towards the growth of local economies as an economic multiplier, which generates positive outcomes for the locals. Apart from that, the food industry also invests in newer innovations when it comes to the future of the food industry,

Statistical Process Control for the Food Industry: A Guide for Practitioners and Managers, First Edition.
Sarina Abdul Halim Lim and Jiju Antony.

which results in better research and development outcomes for the food industry (Unnevehr 2017). Research also enables the food industry suppliers and manufacturers to invest in more sustainable ways of manufacturing fresh produce while ensuring that the impact on the environment is less for a better future.

An increase in food exports also increases international trade relationships between countries since there are more opportunities for the exchange of different raw or processed food, to a greater number of destinations around the world (Unnevehr 2017). Increasing technology enables the food to be processed and packaged safely for long distance distribution.

Furthermore, developing countries have shown a higher interest in processed food products due to the increasing demand for newer types of foods. The huge demand and supply of food manufacturers and suppliers have enabled a diversified supply of food, including the quality and price of food supply. This also allows food to be more affordable for those who are not able to spend on expensive food. Having a wide range of alternatives also means that people have more choices and can choose different types of food based on their willingness to try out different and new products, or choose the price range with which they are comfortable. This gives customers more purchasing power.

2.2   What Is the Role of Food Industry in the Global Context?

The food industry has a role in the expansion of opportunities and economic growth locally and globally, from family units, communities, small and medium enterprises, and international corporation (Pfitzer and Krishnaswamy 2007).

Figure 2.1 shows the opportunity of the food industry in being an economic contributor for those in the industry. Farmers start by growing crops and fresh produce such as fruits and vegetables for their own consumption. The additional produce is then exchanged at local community markets among farmers and the people. Then, small businesses package this produce to send it to nearby locations such as fresh farmers' markets and local grocery stores and supermarkets. This then turns into national supply as businesses start expanding the supply of fresh produce to more locations in and around the country. Finally, international supermarket chains and brands then further market and package the products for international exports.

The process of food packaging and distribution creates many job opportunities, not only for the farmers, but also for the local businesses that supply this fresh produce. Furthermore, exporting fresh produce from one country to another widens the scope of the market and distribution numbers, which increases sales and the growing demand also increases the revenue for the food suppliers. International chains that participate in the selling and distribution of

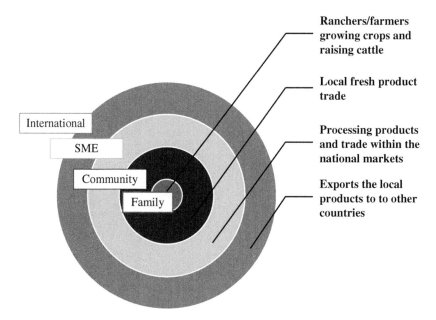

Figure 2.1 Food as an economic opportunity.

local produce must have enough understanding of local demands and markets (Pfitzer and Krishnaswamy 2007). Furthermore, companies should also be able to ensure the consistent quality of the food being supplied, and to ensure that the supply of fresh produce is always increasing to cope with increasing demand locally and internationally. Besides that, international chains also tend to invest for long-term opportunities and benefits for farmers and their families, since this will provide them with long-term opportunities, and help to ensure continuous productivity of fresh produce in the region (Pfitzer and Krishnaswamy 2007).

2.3 Several Classifications of Food Industry from Several Sources

The food industry can be classified into different categories such as agriculture, marketing, food processing, retail and regulations, wholesale and distributions, and manufacturing (New World Encyclopedia 2017). Research and development of newer food types and food processes are also vital in the food industry. Each category is independent in its role with food, as well as being interlinked, since there is a need to work hand-in-hand to achieve the best output for sales and distribution to the general public and to also achieve high quality food supply and manufacturing (Figure 2.2).

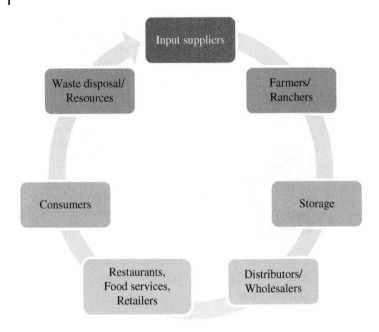

Figure 2.2 The food value chain.

Table 2.1 Comparisons on the classifications and contributions of the food industry in the UK.

Industry/categories	Contribution (£ billion)			
	2014	2015	2016	2017
Food and drink wholesalers	10.7	11.9	10	12.3
Manufacturing (food and beverage)	26.5	26.9	28	29.5
Food and beverage retailing	26.1	30.2	29.5	29.4
Agriculture and fishing	9	10.7	9	9.2
Catering business	26.9	29.1	32	32.7

In the UK, agriculture has been an important aspect of the food industry, with a total contribution of more than 14 billion GBP worth of local supplies to the country (Traill 2008). Agricultural exports are reported to be low, while the workforce has employed more than half a million workers, showing a healthy sign of economic contribution to the country (UK). Some of the other key figures and contributions are listed in the table below (Table 2.1).

The food chain and supply are a substantial component of all national economy. Food and beverages manufacturing in the UK contribute the second largest output compared to other manufacturing sectors.

In the first stage of farm production, the production of food is mainly raw and fresh, with minimum processing (e.g. the production of fruits and vegetables). UK farms supply relatively three-quarters of its raw material. There is a threat from the UK sourced food supply to the manufacturing industry when financial returns to primary producers are low and there are deteriorating levels of farm subsidy (Bourlakis and Weightman 2008). The contribution of food manufacturers can be quantified in several categories:

- Gross national product;
- proportion of consumer expenditure;
- imports and exports of food on balance of payments;
- number of employed workers; and
- value added.

The UK food manufacturers are expected to consistently and efficiently produce quality food. The food manufacturers play a critical role in the supply chain being the mediator of producer and retailer and carrying the primary role in delivering quality products. At this stage, the processing begins to transform raw food materials into different forms. This can involve sugar refining processes, as well as the processing of grains to produce flour. In the second stage of processing, food is further processed to be readily eaten by freezing food items. This creates ready to eat food items such as ice creams and frozen meals. In the fourth stage, food products are then distributed to different parts of the country, to different wholesalers and retailers. Finally, consumers purchase these products to be consumed from supermarkets and retail shops (Unnevehr 2017).

According to Zokaei and Simons (2006), the supply chain does not give customers the opportunity to customise food products, and does not give the opportunity for farmers to meet directly with customer's changing requirements. The effectiveness of the food value chain has to be measured in terms of satisfying customer's needs and wants through the efficient management of the food chain. Therefore, there exists a gap between the supply of food and customer wants. Compared to the past, the food manufacturers have closer relationships with their customers and the retailers where they increase their demands to their suppliers for quality assured and economical produce. On the other hands, it is clear that the key stakeholders in the food chain are the farmers and food producers, government, scientific committee and consumers as shown in Figure 2.3 below.

The producers are focused on the production of food primarily through farming, while also focused on research to find new ways of improving production.

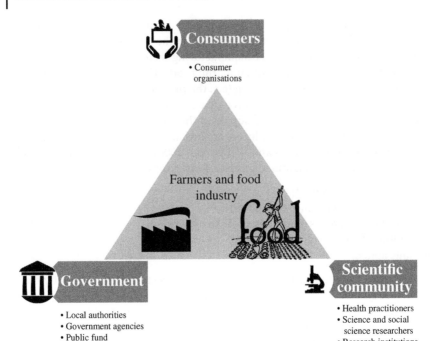

Figure 2.3 Stakeholders in the food chain.

The processors would primarily be focused on manufacturing and altering raw food materials through multiple processors. This would then be handed over to the distributors who are focused on distributing and selling the food products. Consumers would then buy and consume the products based on considerations such as pricing and branding. Lastly, the regulators are the government and the non-governmental organisations who focus on food safety and public policies to ensure the safety of food manufacturing. These stakeholders all play a role in the food chain, and function with each other to ensure the smooth flow of food production from raw materials to processed and completed food (Deloitte 2013). The disruption of the food chain is typically caused by the risk of hazard of the product.

2.4 How is the Food Industry Different from Other Industries?

According to Murray (2007), the food industry differs from other industries as the product (food as the raw material) can be processed into a different form and sold to consumers. For instance, produce from the farm can be processed into a packaged or canned food or sold in the raw state as it was produced. Furthermore, in some cases, the food is sourced, put together and frozen, only to be reheated when needed. This changes the economic income growth and contribution, as sales and distribution can continue to happen when food is repackaged or changed (Murray 2007). Apart from that, the different components and ingredients for food, can be sourced from different parts of the world to be put together for a single dish. For instance, a bowl of noodles may contain some local ingredients, imported cured meat, and maybe some imported ingredients sourced from a particular region (Murray 2007). This shows a close dependent relationship between food suppliers and manufacturers, as well as those who use it for daily operations such as in restaurants and hotels around the world.

The food industry is also expected to grow at a rapid rate, especially in developing economies around the world (Murray 2007). Branded supermarket and hypermarket chains, particularly from Europe and the United States have increased their presence in developing countries, making food even more affordable and accessible for growing populations. This also means that people are more exposed to different types of food, and this only increases the food industry around the world. This in turn increases the competitiveness among the different food manufacturers and suppliers, since there would be more pressure to produce and manufacture better quality produce, and use more sustainable methods of producing food supplies to ensure long-term business outcomes for local food businesses (Murray 2007).

2.5   Customers and Consumers

The end user in the food chain is the consumer, where the challenge for the food supply chain is to satisfy and meet consumer needs and expectations. Therefore, there is a variety of research from government and commercial businesses explaining the habits of consumers (e.g. National Food Survey taking a snapshot of the consumers purchasing behaviour). Faced with derived demand and dependent on the end user, such information is critical to FSM players to monitor general demand, aware of the trends and changes over time, reaction to price and get a big picture in terms of food consumption. Another source of information is from the commercial research which provide only selected information describing the consumption and purchase behaviour of product categories and individual brands. Information from the commercial research is patented where the information is not for public (people outside the organisation). In buying the products, consumers make judgements on certain key attributes to decide how well the products satisfy their requirements and needs and the advantageous of the products or brand compared to others.

There are general models describing the factors affecting food purchasing behaviour. A comprehensive model was developed to consider the relationship between personal characteristics, food products, and environmental characteristics. Most of the food business focused on the sensory evaluations as the quality characteristics to represent the customer voice. The model is product focused on the relationship between taste and flavour in relation to the other influences. These food quality models reflected consumers' voice as it is a critical part of food chain. The standards for quality in food contain four common areas, which are the legal standards, voluntary label standards, industry standards, and consumer standards. The consumer standards represent the key requirements towards a product and it is the experience used by the industry for consumers.

2.6 Government Plan

As one of the main and important guidelines, the UK government has introduced a national plan for several purposes. For instance, the Department for Environment Food and Rural Affairs prepare Food Chain – Evidence Plan 2013/2014–2017/2018. The sustainable food policy is set within a wider national policy with coalition priorities and it addresses the ministries priorities:

- Food businesses to have a better environmental performance to improve productivity and competitiveness of the business;
- to promote a sustainable approach to the use of materials and management of waste throughout society; and
- to implement an impartial approach to regulation and remove unnecessary burdens.

The government also outlined the International Action Plan 2016–2020 for the UK food and drink industry to accelerate UK export growth and to increase confidence for the businesses interested in exporting. The key strategic objectives are through raising ambition, increasing capability, and identifying opportunities.

2.7 Summary

- It is a competitive industry, of which comprises 96% of the industry are SMEs.
- The food industry is also expected to grow at a rapid rate, especially in developing economies around the world.
- The food industry is unique to other industries, as its products can be processed into a different form and sold to consumers.

- Food industry is a complex and multitiered system starting from producers and ending with the consumers.
- The UK food chain comprises five key stakeholders, which are the producers, processors, distributors, consumers, and the regulators.
- The food industry contributes towards the growth of local economies and generates positive outcomes for local businesses.
- The huge demand and supply of food manufacturers and suppliers have enabled a diversified supply of food, including the quality and price of food supply.

3

Quality and Safety in the Food Industry

3.1 Introduction

This chapter provides an overview of the concepts and practices correlate with safety and quality in the food industry that is based on:

- Government regulations
- Requirements and expectations of customers and consumers

These regulations and requirement impacted the changes in food industry operations including significant developments in food quality and food safety activities. The continual efforts to the basic need of food quality and food safety influenced by numerous factors:

- Consumer expectations relating to various aspects of food (e.g. nutrition, convenience, additives)
- Incidents relating to food safety
- Environmental concerns
- Changes in government regulatory processes
- Traceability in food production and processing
- Technological changes
- Foods derived from biotechnology
- Irradiated foods
- Food security issues
- Organic foods
- Economic factors
- Issues relating to international trade

In every country, food business can be operated on different levels such as local, national, or multinational corporations, which use either intensive farming or industrial agriculture in maximising productivity.

Industry has adopted safety and quality systems that have been developed customised for the application of the food industry. The current environment of the industry is witness to the fact that food companies are committed to

Statistical Process Control for the Food Industry: A Guide for Practitioners and Managers, First Edition.
Sarina Abdul Halim Lim and Jiju Antony.
© 2019 John Wiley & Sons Ltd. Published 2019 by John Wiley & Sons Ltd.

safety as they employ robust food safety programs that not only meet the requirements of the law, but also go beyond the requirements. Accordingly, the requirements in food quality and food safety are addressed through the use of quality management systems and programs that include quality assurance, quality control, and the Hazard Analysis and Critical Control Point (HACCP) system, Good Manufacturing Practice (GMP), British Retail Consortium (BRC) and Food Safety System Certification (FSSC 22000). Within a particular food company, the food quality and food safety activities are likely to be covered by some combination of these programs or systems.

With an understanding of the importance of food safety certifications which has impacted not only towards the law and regulations compliance, but also for marketing strategy, the industry has quickly adapted to HACCP principles. Even those companies that are in non-HACCP-regulated industries have also embraced those principles. Preaching the idea of the food safety program, most companies go to the extent of developing supplier inspection programs. They are required to divide samples and perform laboratory analysis and third-party external audits.

It takes diligence every day. It's not just talk; it's action behind the talk.
(Joan Menke-Schaenzer, ConAgra)

In the industry, the terms of food quality and food safety are often used inter-changeably. However, it is important for the food industry practitioners and experts to identify the differences between those two. In general, food quality is the degree to which all the requirements established are being met. Food safety is the extent of the ability of a company to conform to those requirements relating to characteristics that have the potential to be the cause of illness or injury. It is clear that the food business that does not comply with the food safety requirements automatically does not conform to the food quality requirements. However, a food product may conform to the requirement of food safety but fail to conform to the other quality requirements. A clear distinction between food quality and food safety should be emphasised because priority should be given to protecting consumers from food-borne illnesses or harm.

Although the food industry is aware of negative public opinion, not all companies are committed to improving the industry's image
(Hubbard 2003)

A key feature of the food industry is that food producers must comply with the market demand and law and regulations to satisfy both safety and quality criteria for their products. Therefore, food producers should decide the most suitable quality management system for their specific activity and establish effective systems for managing quality and safety of their products.

3.2   Food Quality

In defining food quality, the customer's perceptions of food quality are crucial and need to be emphasised. It is the level to which all the established criteria relating to the characteristics of food are met. In the industry, quality of the food can be referred to in two dimensions which are objectives and subjective quality. Quality of the food also depends on the degree the product characteristics meet the consumer preferences. Quality not only depends on objective characteristics of the product but also on consumers' perception of satisfying personal requirements and objectives.

3.2.1   Objective and Subjective Quality

The objective quality of the food refers to the physical characteristics created in the product by the engineers and food technologists. Meanwhile, a quality that is perceived by the consumers is considered as the subjective quality (Grunert 2005). The association between the dimensions above is at the centre of the economic importance of quality:

→ food producers interpret consumer expectations into physical product characteristics
→ consumers can then deduce desired qualities based on the way the product is designed
→ quality is a competitive parameter for food producers.

From the holistic model of food quality, food safety is a subset of food quality, at least to the degree that consumers perceive food safety as the necessary characteristic. Common examples of quality characteristics of food, excluding the food safety characteristics, are:

• Declared gross or net quantity (e.g. weight or volume) of a unit of the food or net fill of a food container
• Declared or claimed amount of one or more stated components of a food
• Chemical composition
• Appearance (e.g. size, shape, colour)
• Flavour
• Aroma
• Texture
• Viscosity
• Shelf-life stability
• Fitness for use as human food
• Wholesomeness
• Adulteration
• Packaging
• Labelling

The definition of food quality, three proposed types of food quality; product-oriented quality, process-oriented quality, and user-oriented quality.

- Product-oriented quality is concerned about a food product's physical properties, like fat percentage and cell content in milk.
- Process-oriented quality related to the degree where it is concerned with the extent of the quality characteristics of the products which maintain a product stable at targeted levels (product specification limits).
- The user-oriented quality is the perception of the customer (intermediate user or end user or even retailers) towards the products.

Most of the quality characteristics are listed in the Food Act and regulations in most countries, which make it inevitable for the companies to work towards achieving the quality characteristics. For example, food producers that fail to meet regulatory requirements relating to a standard of declared quantity, declared ingredients, or label claims, can be penalised as making fraud and misbranding. Regarding its safety and shelf-life, the spoilage, deterioration, or decomposition of foods, production of a harmful substance that can lead to illness or death, are all perceived as a failure to offer a product fit for human consumption.

Scoping down the definition of food quality, it is known that to define food quality is going to be complex. A model which was developed by Grunert et al. (1995), to depict a framework of the dimension of food quality. The model suggests two approaches to analyse food perception; which offer the time dimension (horizontal) and inference making dimension (vertical).

- *The time dimension.* Differentiates quality perception before and after purchase.
  The dimension covers the distinction between search, experience, and credence qualities and its implications for consumer's ability to assess quality before and purchase. It also covers the assumption that the extent of confirmation of pre-purchase quality expectations will determine consumer satisfaction and repurchase intention.
- *The consumer's inference-making dimension.* Focus on the consumers' approach to infer quality from several different signals and on the behaviour of the consumers to choose the food product properties that are desirable.

This is done by linking the product properties to basic motivators of human behaviour. The concept of confidence in inference-making is believed to be linked to the consumers' knowledge and expertise.

Following the definition by Codex Alimentarius on the food suitability as the assurance that food is acceptable for human consumption, this includes criteria such as wholesomeness, and extraneous matter. The quality requirements are not solely developed by the government; many criteria for food quality characteristics are also outlined by the customers and consumers' expectation.

3.3   Food Safety

The food industry accounted for both legal and moral responsibility for serving to customers and consumers safe and quality food. Food safety is a critical aspect of public policy, and it has for some years figured prominently on the political agenda. Food safety is a part of food quality. A food product that is of good quality can be considered safe to be consumed, however a safe product may not necessarily be perceived as a quality food product (Figure 3.1).

It can be specifically defined as the possibility of not contracting a disease due to consuming a certain food, and it is a concept based on the objective risk assessment by the scientists and food experts. The safety paradigm is that although the food is safer, consumers' attitude and subjective assessment is subjugated by high levels of ambiguity. The endorsed food laws and regulations by the government around the world designed to ensure that foods are fit for human consumption. Food law does not only protect consumers from harm or unsafe foods, but also from fraud relating to specific established food quality characteristics.

Figure 3.1 Food quality and food safety.

The primary purpose of such enactment is to protect consumers from harmful foods and from resulting from misrepresentation or fraud relating to specific established food quality characteristics. Mostly in each country, governments established several agencies to foresee and enforce the food laws and regulations to secure customers confidence with the safety of the food in the current market. The regulatory response can be through enforcement of food safety standards; no direct effect on consumer food buying behaviour, but is arguably regarding economic efficiency when consumer preferences for safety are presumed to be heterogeneous. Another regulatory response requires endeavours for providing transparency and educates consumers to develop their judgements on food safety through a consumer awareness programme and consumer information instruments (e.g. labelling). In recent years, the general public has become more critical with processes involved in the food production – starting at the farm level and the processing level.

Typically, in a food company, overall responsibility for the effective implementation and continuous application of these programs are delegated to the senior management. Food safety practices have always been integrated into quality assurance system or quality management system; therefore, these systems can address both food quality and food safety aspects.

The challenge is the food producers often fail to provide sufficient food safety programme as it is considered costly for the companies to run food safety tests and some may be unable to certify the safety of foods provided the vast array of microbial agents that have the potential for hazard along the food production process. Therefore, the governments around the world took serious action by emphasising the application of systematic approaches to ensure the safety of the food products (e.g. mandate the implementation of HACCP system in the food industry).

3.4   Hazard Analysis and Critical Control Point (HACCP)

3.4.1   Concept

The HACCP system is widely acknowledged food safety management system and its becoming the international tool focused on prevention of problems to assure the food products that are safe to consume. It provides a systematic and scientific but common-sense application of technical and scientific principles to the food production process from harvest to consumption. It involves in all phases of food production (e.g. food preparation, food processing, consumer handling, foodservice, retail and distribution).

HACCP

HACCP is a system based on prevention of hazards to the industry to produce safe food to consumers, instead of inspection.

The food producers, distributors and retailers required sufficient information about the food, procedures and processes involved in producing food, so they will be able to determine the points that caused food safety problem; called as critical control point (CCP). Prevention is easier if 'how' and 'where' are known to efficiently control and avoid the hazard contamination.

As it was defined, HACCP concept covers all types of potential food safety hazards – biological, chemical and physical – whether they are naturally occurring by the environment or generated by a mistake in the manufacturing process or handling. HACCP is designed to prevent food hazards which can be categorised as microbiological, chemical and physical hazards.

The system is outlined by seven principles that involved identification and assessment of the severity of hazards and their risks (hazard analysis) that related with growth, harvesting, processing, manufacture, distribution, marketing, preparation and/or use of a raw material or food product (Figure 3.2).

Figure 3.2 Steps in implementing HACCP.

HACCP has become internationally well known as the best approach of ensuring food safety. The production of meat, poultry, seafood and juice have been mandated to apply HACCP by the US food regulatory body. The European Union (EU) also adopted several new regulations on the hygiene of foods, including one (852/2004/EC) directing that as of January 1, 2006, all food business implement procedures in food production based on HACCP principles. Government from other countries, Canada, Japan and Australia, have adopted or are adopting HACCP-based food safety control systems (Bernard and Scott 2007).

3.4.2 HACCP Principles

A food safety management system based on the HACCP principles will ensure the identification of hazards and to be controlled to avoid the risk of food safety.

3.4.2.1 Principle 1
Identify any hazards that must be prevented eliminated or reduced. This can be done by preparing the list of steps in the process where the critical hazards may occur and describe the preventive measures.

3.4.2.2 Principle 2
Identify the CCPs at the steps at which control is essential in the process. A CCP is a step at which control can be applied and is vital to prevent the hazard of food safety or reduce it to an acceptable level. The application of a decision tree can facilitate the determination of a CCP. A 'step' defined as any stage in food production or manufacture including raw materials, their receipt and production, harvesting, transport, formulation, processing, storage. For instance, raw meat, it will kill pathogens such as *Escherichia coli* 0157.

3.4.2.3 Principle 3
Establish critical limits at CCPs for preventive measures associated with each identified CCP. Limit for CCP is a standard which distinguishes acceptability from unacceptability. The limits indicate the maximum or minimum value to the hazards (physical, biological, or chemical) and it must be controlled at a CCP to prevent, eliminate, or reduce the food safety hazard at the acceptance value. The parameters for the CCP limits should be measurable such as time, temperature, humidity, water activity and pH value.

3.4.2.4 Principle 4
Establish procedures to monitor the CCPs. Monitoring is the core component in the HACCP system. The results of monitoring are used to establish procedures to adjust the process and maintain control. Monitoring is a strategic order of observations to assess whether a CCP is in-control and to provide

correct records for future use in verification. Monitoring can provide warnings to the manufacturers if there is pattern towards loss of control so that before it exceeded the limit, action can be taken. The responsible staff for the monitoring procedure should be adequately trained.

3.4.2.5   Principle 5

If a CCP is not-in-control, implement corrective actions. The management should provide a corrective action plan as a standard operating procedure if there is a violation at the CCP. Corrective action is an action took place when the CCP has exceeded the limit, i.e. a loss of control. The plant management has to determine the corrective action in advance. The employees monitoring the CCP should understand this process and be trained to perform the appropriate corrective actions.

3.4.2.6   Principle 6

Establish procedures to verify whether the above procedures include supplementary tests and procedures to confirm that HACCP is working effectively. Verification concern the application of procedures, methods, assessments and other evaluations, besides to monitoring, to ensure the compliance with the HACCP plan. Verification can be the calibration of process monitoring instruments at specified intervals, direct observation of monitoring, and corrective actions. Other methods of verification are sampling of product, monitoring records review and inspections can serve to verify the HACCP system. The manufacturers must ensure the employees are keeping accurate and timely HACCP records.

3.4.2.7   Principle 7

Establish documents and records concerning all procedures and records appropriate to these principles and their application. Maintaining accurate and complete HACCP records essential for:

- documentation of the HACCP plan compliance;
- solving problem; tracing history of an ingredient, processing of a product, or a finished product
- detecting trends in the selected operation that could result in a deviation
- identifying and narrowing a product recall.

Despite the widespread interest for HACCP, some of the controversies circulating its application is whether HACCP is effective in eliminate the food safety hazards and whether it allows the food producers to meet the food safety objectives in the most efficient approach. HACCP provides a systematic way of identifying food safety hazards and making sure that they are being controlled day-in, day-out. The management can apply the widely known PDCA (Plan, Do, Check and Act) as a systematic template to execute the HACCP plan as described in the Figure 3.3.

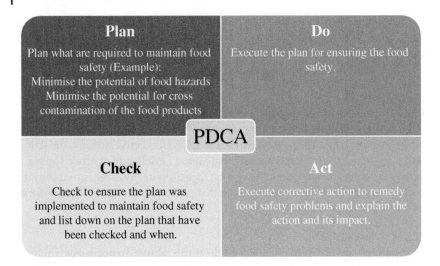

Plan	Do
Plan what are required to maintain food safety (Example): Minimise the potential of food hazards Minimise the potential for cross contamination of the food products	Execute the plan for ensuring the food safety.

PDCA

Check	Act
Check to ensure the plan was implemented to maintain food safety and list down on the plan that have been checked and when.	Execute corrective action to remedy food safety problems and explain the action and its impact.

Figure 3.3 PDCA for HACCP implementation.

3.4.3 Hazards

The seven principles of HACCP focus on the detection and control of microbiological, chemical and physical hazards in the processing and production of the food. The hazard assessment and the routine monitoring of critical control measures should be well documented to provide the basis for audit checks and may provide evidence of due diligence in the event of legal action. Careful and thorough implementation of HACCP principles by the operators demonstrates their commitment to food safety; improves employee awareness of their role in protecting consumers, and accentuates management's responsibility for the safety of the food they are producing.

3.4.3.1 Physical Contamination

Adulteration is one of the major physical contaminations. It is the mixing of low-grade material with the superior materials for product, subsequently reducing the quality (taste, colour, odour and nutritional value) that later on causing ill effects on the health of the consumer (Hurst and Harris 2013). Most of the food products sold in the market has the potential to physical contamination, but according Lucey (2006), food production that are heavily adulterated are milk products, edible oil, spices, beverages drinks, sweets, pulses, sugar, processed foods, rice and cereal products like flour (Lucey 2006). Although chemical hazards are still dreaded by many consumers and the consumers most commonly identified physical hazards, microbiological hazards are the most serious from public health perspective. Therefore, while HACCP address the three types of hazards, majority of the focus is focused on microbiological hazard.

3.4.3.2 Chemical Contamination

It is widely known that chemical has elicit harmful effects when living things consumed as it is said to be toxic. The application of chemicals in the food production and processing may impacted the food quality and dangerously disguises the deterioration and constitutes deliberate adulteration that can cause injuries to the consumers. The chemical hazards can be separated into three categories:

- Naturally occurred.
- Intentionally added.
- Accidently added

The presence of a chemical may not always cause hazard. However, it is the amount of the chemical determines whether it can cause injuries or not. It is advised that food additives (preservatives, colouring artificial sweetening, antioxidants, emulsifiers, flavours enhancers), if used should be of approved quality and processed under GMPs (Edith and Ochubiojo 2012). There are also chemicals that are used on food processing equipment such as sanitizer or oil applied on the equipment.

3.4.3.3 Microbiological Contamination

Contamination of food is the most dominant health problem in the modern world. These organisms can affect human health, including infection, intoxication and the worst case is death. Microbiological criteria should be established and ensure the food is free of pathogenic microorganisms to secure the quality and safety of the food. Microbiological hazards can occur at any stages of food production or processing, including the raw materials, ingredients and finished products. Pathogenic microorganisms enter food processing from several main routes: the external environment, people, raw materials, and equipment and vehicles.

Microorganisms may be beneficial, end even essential. However, some can be pathogenic. It is this category of microorganism that concerns food processors and public health officials.

Pathogens can be temporary or sporadic visitors, or they may persist for long periods. Therefore, the microbiological assessment of the food products has to be adopted throughout the critical area of the food production. Food companies need to prepare, define and apply the microbiological criteria ensure clear distinction safe and unsafe food.

Food poisoning often occurred due to the consumption of used, residual, fermented or spoiled food, as these may be contaminated with bacteria or other microorganisms, hence toxic. These toxins are very difficult to eliminate as they survive normal cooking temperatures. Inadequate refrigerated food contaminated with microorganism such as *Clostridium perfringens* (breeds in the alimentary canal producing the poisoning within 8–12 hours after the ingestion of contaminated food) is one of the major causes of food poisoning. Some of the lethal effects of microbial contamination of food include; liver cancer (aflatoxin), Flavism (hemolytic anaemia) (consume broad beans or by inhaling the pollen of its flower).

3.4.4 Documentation

Documents should always be updated as they offer information on the events happening and decisions and action taken. Where visual monitoring is necessary, for example to ensure carcasses are free of visible faecal contamination, records can be limited to 'exception reporting'. A record is only made when there is a problem or something uncommon happens and confirming the corrective action taken as the feedback action.

3.4.5 Critical Control Point (CCP)

As of today, HACCP has become the most reliable and cost-effective method to ensure food safety. However, common danger is when the company has properly validated and implement a HACCP plan, the team tends to view that the challenging task of guaranteeing the food safety of the product is over. However, realistically, this is only the beginning. The biggest challenges is to sustain the HACCP application in a day-to-day basis in the production. Therefore, having to plan the HACCP, an effective process control approach is vital.

Typically, quality control operation (identification and control of critical control points) enable the compliance during operation.

3.4.6 How to Do it?

3.4.6.1 Step 1: Develop HACCP Team
HACCP is a system that should be developed to a specific product and process which it can covers from harvesting/processing raw materials, food manufacturing to the point of consumption. Food companies that have the intention to apply HACCP certification are required to develop system using a standardised approach that are outlined in a series of steps.

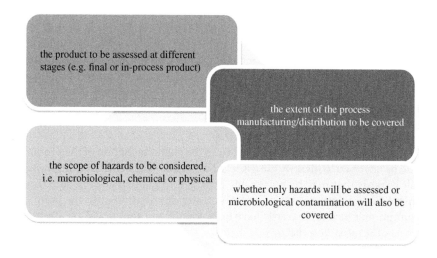

Figure 3.4 Target of HACCP implementation.

The role of the team is to carry out a HACCP assessment, develop a HACCP plan and implement the HACCP system. The team developed should be a multidisciplinary and consist of representative from each function concerned with the manufacture and distribution of the product:

- Quality assurance technologist/microbiologist – fully familiar with the quality and safety requirements for the product, potential hazards and risk,
- Production specialist – conversant with the product manufacturing and packing processes
- Distribution specialist – fully familiar with the processes of storage and distribution through which product passes between the points of packed product storage and sale to the consumer
- Food engineer – fully conversant with the design, operation and performance of the plant and equipment

The senior management should ensure the team members are aware and understand the direction of the HACCP implementation in the company towards the team members (Figure 3.4).

3.4.6.2 Step 2: Describe and Characterise the Product

A detail evaluation should be made of the product's characteristics, prescribed storage conditions and recommended use, identifying as relevant. Example of the characteristics are ingredients, water activity, pH, temperature, ingredients, shelf-life, humidity, standard pattern of use, instruction to consumers.

3.4.6.3   Step 3: Construct the Process Flow Diagram

A step-by-step flow diagram of the process should be established, covering the agreed scope of the HACCP system. Engineering drawings and manufacturing process conditions should be included to supplement the development of process-flow diagrams. The HACCP team should verify the processing operation in the flow diagram at all stages and hours of operation, which then the team will amend the flow diagram where applicable.

3.4.6.4   Step 4: Identify the Hazards Control

The information and the data collected from the characterisation of the product should be analysed to identify the associated hazards. The HACCP team should list all hazards that may be reasonably expected to happen at each step from main production, processing, manufacture, and distribution until the point of consumption. Once the hazards have been identified they should be assessed in terms of severity and risk.

3.4.6.5   Step 5: Quantify and Analyse the Hazards

The assessment of severity, being the magnitude of consequences resulting from a hazard, enables the team to realise the status and importance of the hazard in terms of the overall HACCP. According to Early (2012), there are three stages of severity of the hazards (high severity, medium severity and low severity) (Figure 3.5).

Figure 3.3 shows that the risks, being the probability of occurrence of a hazard, can also be categorised as high, medium and low. High risk depicted an expectation that the hazard will occur, medium risk indicates that there is a

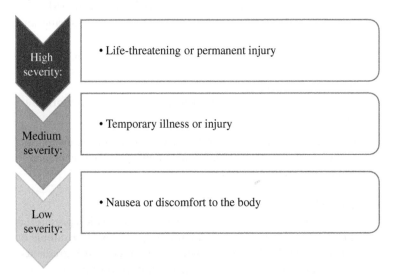

Figure 3.5 Severity of hazards.

reasonable chance that it will occur and low risk indicates that the occurrence will be rare.

Hazard analysis consists of an assessment of all procedures related to the production, distribution, raw material and food process and production as overall. The assessment is objectively to:

- identify potentially hazardous raw materials and food (contain poisonous substances, pathogens, large number of food spoilage microorganisms)
- identify occurrences of hazards and severity of their adverse health effects
- investigate the survival or multiplication of microorganisms of concern
- production or persistence in foods of toxins, chemicals or physical agents;
- identify conditions leading to contaminations
- identify the potential sources and specific points of contamination
- determine the probability that microorganisms will survive or multiply during production, processing, distribution, storage and preparation for consumption
- assess the risks and severity of hazards identified.

3.4.6.6 Step 6: Identify Control Requirements, Targets and Tolerances

Having identified the hazards and established their importance through the assessment of severity and risk, control requirements should be identified. With the control requirements identified, the targets and critical limits for control should be established. Control can only be considered to be achieved with the elimination of a hazard or its reduction to a level within the tolerance.

3.4.6.7 Step 7: Identify CCPs and Assess Existing Controls

There may be more than one CCP at which control is applied to address the same hazard. The determination of a CCP in the HACCP system can be facilitated by the application of a decision tree (Figure 3.6) which indicates a logic reasoning approach.

Control requirements, targets and tolerances should be matched to the process-flow information and data to:

- identify the position of CCPs in the process
- confirm whether existing controls at CCPs meet the newly established control requirements
- decide what revisions to existing controls are necessary
- decide how new control requirements are to be applied
- identify whether hazards will be eliminated or reduced by process stages occurring downstream.

CCPs should be numbered, as this aids practical identification. Also, the numbers may be used as cross-references in documents additional to the HACCP documentation. If given a situation that hazard has been detected at

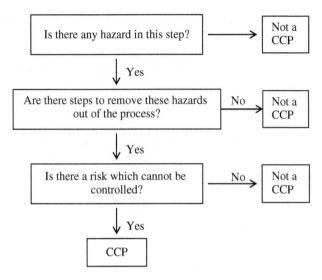

Figure 3.6 Example of tree diagram.

a step where control is essential for safety and quality, and no control measure exists at that step, then the process or the product should be revised at earlier stage to include the control measure in the production process.

3.4.6.8 Step 8: Establish a Monitoring System for Each CCP

Monitoring is a critical scheduled observation activity in HACCP system of a CCP relative to its critical limits, where it confirms that control is being achieved within outlined critical limits. The team should establish criteria for the methods and frequencies of CCP monitoring and the monitoring measures must be able to detect toss of control at the CCP. Monitoring mechanism should ideally provide the information in time to make alterations in preventing the process violating the critical limits.

Where possible, process adjustments should be made when monitoring results indicate a trend towards loss of control at a CCP. The corrective action should be taken before a deviation occurs. The data from monitoring must be evaluated by person with knowledge and authority to carryout corrective actions when indicated. Most monitoring procedures for CCPs will need to be done rapidly because they relate to on-line processes and there will insufficient time for lengthy analytical testing.

3.5 Good Manufacturing Practice

GMP is a system to ensure that the products are consistently produced controlled according to quality standards. GMP are required by several regulations around the world, especially United States Food Department Agency (FDA) 21CFR174.5 and EU Commission Regulation (EC) No 2023/2006. Though GMP is not a Statistical tool of quality control, it is inherent in food quality control system and forms an important part of the overall as the food safety system.

There is a major emphasis on compliance with GMP in all related food legislation and food safety certification standards. Every food product under the GMP system must:

- consistently high quality
- be fitting to their intended use
- meet the requirements of the food act and legislation or product specification

---

It should be noted that the FDA regulations for Good Manufacturing Practice is modified from time to time, and it is necessary to periodically review quality control procedures to insure compliance.

The GMP requirements are made in general to allow flexibility and individual variation by different manufacturers to implement the requirements suits with their needs. GMP covers seven subsections for avoiding these possibilities in the following general areas:

3.5.1 Personnel

Cleanliness, education and training, disease control and supervision.

Personnel with diseases or other conditions that potentially contaminate food are to be excluded from manufacturing operations. This section outlines requirements with regards to personal hygiene, removal of jewellery and other hazardous objects, application of glove and hair net, appropriate storage of personal items, and restrictions on various activities, such as eating and smoking. It is required to have appropriate and sufficient food safety training.

3.5.2 Plant and Grounds

This section requires that plants be built to minimise the potential for contamination. Good equipment storage, property surrounding maintenance, effective management, storage, segregate potential operations potentially to occur contamination, sanitation precautions for outside fermentation vessels, building construction to permit adequate cleaning, sufficient lighting, ventilation and airing.

3.5.3 Sanitary Operation

Building and Fixtures: maintenance, cleaning and sanitising to prevent contamination. Special precautions for toxic sanitising agents. Food contact surfaces: sanitation procedures. Sanitise physical facilities and utilities in a way that keep away the food contamination. The section also outlined pest control and cleaning management includes types of food contact surfaces and the frequency of the cleaning activities.

3.5.4 Sanitary Facilities and Controls

Water supply, plumbing, sewage disposal, toilet and hand-washing facilities, handwashing facilities, rubbish and offal disposal.

3.5.5 Equipment and Utensils

This part outlined the requirements for the design, construction, and maintenance of equipment and utensils to guarantee sanitary conditions. Materials and workmanship are cleanable, safe against contamination toxic, and appropriately maintained. This section also describes specific requirement; automated temperature control and alarm system to alert employees towards drastic change in temperature.

3.5.6 Processes and Controls

This section lists the general sanitation processes and controls necessary to ensure that food is suitable for human consumption. Thorough sanitation plan in receiving inspection, transporting, separating, manufacturing, packaging, and storing. Appropriate quality control operations and food packaging to assure that food is fit for human consumption.

3.5.7 Raw Materials

The raw materials are required to be inspected for processing into food and stored properly to minimise deterioration. Containers shall be inspected for possible contamination or deterioration of food. Levels of toxins and detection of pest contamination or extraneous material should comply with food law, regulations, and guidelines. Avoidance of contamination is important at storage of raw materials or rework. Frozen raw materials shall be thawed only as required prior to use and protected from adulteration.

Best GMP programme considered the whole production chain of food contact material and products:

- Selection of the materials
- Incoming raw material quality control
- Storage
- Production equipment cleaning procedures
- Manufacturing facility housekeeping procedure
- Material traceability
- Product QA and QC control
- Management of change
- Employees training
- Product packaging
- Storage and shipping

Manufacturing, packaging and storage to be organised for protecting from microorganism growth. It also addresses the monitoring of critical points of physical parameters such as time, flow rate, temperature, humidity and pH. Growth of microorganisms shall be inhibited by refrigeration, freezing, acidity, sterilising, irradiating and control. Guidelines and manuals for blanching should be prepared focusing on thermophilic bacteria control. Adulterated food, ingredients or raw materials shall be segregated and, if reconditioned, shall be proven to be effectively free from adulteration. Mechanical manufacturing steps shall be executed without contamination. Similar to the food act and regulations, the manual forbids sharing manufacturing space for human and non-human food grade animal feed (or inedible products).

3.5.8   Warehousing and Distribution

Storage and transportation of finished foods shall be protected against physical, chemical and microbial contamination, as well as deterioration of the food and the container.

Food processing companies with sufficient staff might consider incorporating the GMP regulation in the quality control manual, and conducting routine audits to assure conformance. Consulting firms are available to perform periodic GMP inspections for smaller organisations. In either case, a file of satisfactory audits could prove invaluable in the event of suspected product failure resulting in litigation.

3.6 Food and Drug Administration (FDA)

The Food and Drug Administration is a body that accountable for protecting the community health. They ensure the safety, value, biological products and security of drugs, and medical devices. It also ensured the safety of the food supply, cosmetics, and products that emit radiation. Besides food and drugs, FDA also responsible in regulating the manufacturing, marketing, and distribution of tobacco products to ensure the safety of public health and to avoid tobacco use by minors.

FDA is responsible for improving the public health through the innovations for more effective, safer, and more affordable medical products. The agency provides the public the science-based and correct information in regards to the medical products usage and foods consumption to improve or maintain their health.

It ensures the safety of all food except for meat, poultry and some egg products; ensures the safety and effectiveness of all drugs, biological products (including blood, vaccines and tissues for transplantation), medical devices, and animal drugs and feed; and makes sure that cosmetics and medical and consumer products that emit radiation do no harm. One aspect of its jurisdiction over food is regulation of the content of health claims on food labels.

3.7 Summary

- In the food industry, food quality is viewed by the consumers subjectively or objectively through several quality characteristics.
- Food quality can be defined from the customer's dimension, process dimension and production dimension.
- Most common aspect of food quality viewed by the food industry is the safeness of the food as the food producers accounted for both legal and moral responsibility for producing and selling consumers safe and quality food.
- The government endorsed food laws to ensure the food in the market are safe and fit for human consumption.
- HACCP is an international food safety management tool focused on ensuring food is free from hazardous substance (chemical, physical and biological). It contains seven principles that will enable the hazards to be identified.
- GMP is a system to ensure that the products are consistently produced controlled according to quality standards. The GMP outline the requirements for the food producers to ensure food quality at the general areas such as personnel, plant and grounds, sanitary operations, sanitary facilities and controls, equipment and utensils, processes and controls, raw materials and warehousing and distributions.

4

An Introduction of SPC in the Food Industry: Past, Present and Future

4.1 Statistical Process Control: A Brief Overview

Understanding the meaning of Statistical Process Control (SPC) is vital in operating SPC in the food industry. There have been attempts to expand the concept of SPC, beyond the process monitoring technique.

SPC has been categorised into several types of definitions such as:

- technological innovation (Bushe 1988; Roberts, Watson, and Oliver 1989);
- process management technique (Bissell 1994);
- control algorithm (Hryniewicz 1997);
- a component of total quality management (TQM) (Barker 1990);
- one of the quality management system in the food industry (Caswell, Bredahl, and Hooker 1998).
- Wallace et al. (2012) and Davis and Ryan (2005) viewed SPC as a participatory management system – teamwork efforts, employee involvement and enable real-time decision-making to be made (Deming 1986; Elg, Olsson, and Dahlgaard 2008).

> SPC is a powerful collection of problem-solving tools useful in achieving process stability and improving capability through the reduction of variability
>
> (Montgomery 2012)

The focus of SPC is for the users to understand the variation in values of quality characteristics (Woodall 2000). The primary indicator of an effective SPC application is a stable process. The process stability refers to the stability of the underlying probability distribution of a process over time, and these very often can be described as the stability of the distribution parameters over-time (Mahalik and Nambiar 2010). The process stability is extremely crucial as it is one of the pre-requirement to assess the process capability indices determination (Brannstrom-Stenberg and Deleryd 1999; Motorcu and Gullu 2006; Sharma and Kharub 2014).

Statistical Process Control for the Food Industry: A Guide for Practitioners and Managers, First Edition.
Sarina Abdul Halim Lim and Jiju Antony.
© 2019 John Wiley & Sons Ltd. Published 2019 by John Wiley & Sons Ltd.

Prior to the assessment of process capability, the process must be ensured to be stable. Process capability indices developed from an unstable process are not reliable.

Mathematically, of course, we can calculate the capability indices, but for an unstable process, these indices measurements have no real significance, as assignable causes of variations in the process have not been identified. Therefore, correct identification of the type of probability distribution is insufficient without the assurance that the process is statistically stable over time.

4.2 Quality Control in the Food Industry: Before SPC

SPC can be viewed in the form of technology of quality control efforts in the food industry. Quality control had a long history, where it is safe to say since manufacturing industry existed and became competitive, consumers compared products and were continuously searching for a better quality product.

Direction of quality control (QC)
The key purpose of quality control (QC) in the food industry is to ensure the product is consistently produced under a quality standard and is compatible with the market as the product was designed to be sold at a specific price.

We can trace the basics of food quality control, which begin in 2500 BCE wherein Egyptian laws had provisions to prevent meat contamination. Apart from that, people in Athens concentrated on inspecting beer and wines to ensure the purity and soundness of these products (Edith and Ochubiojo 2012).

In the western world, the food industry was one of the earliest industries to be highly dependent on culinary, miller, baker, butcher, and the craftsman on producing food. The Industrial Revolution in England transformed this gradually evolving trend. In the 1820s, the trait of commercialization was reflected through the establishment of the canning industry. However, the quality of the products was dependent on the operator's skills (self-taught) and the canning industry also faced problems with preservation and shelf-life.

It was not until 1840s, the introduction of 'go' tolerance limit was introduced and in 1870s it was transformed to 'go' and 'no-go' tolerance limit. Shewhart and Deming (1939), suggest that the limits (specifications) are the nature of an end requirement on the finished product specified quality characteristics.

The concept 'exact', 'go' and 'no-go'
Manufacturers were aware that they were not capable of making products 'exactly' the same, too costly and unnecessary to make things alike. Therefore, they eased from the term 'exactness' to 'go' and 'no go'.

The term *quality control* is extensively used in engineering terminology. According to Herschdoerfer (1967), it was borrowed by the food industry and has been widely applied in all types of settings. However, it was believed that the food industry can only exercise a similar system if there is quality control from the production of the raw material. Logically in order to have this, the suppliers were required to have a similar control system towards the production of their products (raw materials). Therefore, the trend since the World War II has been that the larger companies are more prone to move towards this direction, compared to the smaller organisations, as there are limits for smaller companies to operate such a system.

In the nineteenth century, the food industry's revolution showed a tremendous expansion by the food industry regarding its production, regulations, and control. Comparatively, in the modern food manufacturing era, the government regulatory body controls and inspects quality levels to ensure that the products meet the standard quality target to meet customer satisfaction.

4.2.1 Inspection! Inspection! Inspection!

An inspection is an organised examination assessment of a formal evaluation exercise. In the case of identified errors during inspections, quality control of the product was limited only to corrective inspection (e.g. it was a way to check the uniformity of the final product by determining the defective products). In 1922, the inspection process was linked formally with quality management, and with the publication of the book 'The Control of Quality in Manufacturing' (Paiva 2013), Shingeo Shingo (1986) defined inspection as a process that involved comparisons with standards. In simple words, it is an effort to detect the 'unacceptable' products or defects found at the end manufacturing process. The standards used during the inspection process, is typically derived from a range of acceptable measurements. Generally, the inspection process is involved in specific functions in the production of food as depicted in the Figure 4.1 below.

The defective products were identified using the current product measurement, which is defined by the quality parameters against the acceptable range measurement. In this industry, defects were produced due to the result of human error, poor quality raw materials and, incorrect packaging material. Shingeo (1986) distinguished types of inspection as:

- judgement inspections (discovering defects after analysing the facts);
- informative inspections (feedback mechanism for correcting the process, e.g. output control charts)
- source inspections (preventing defects before they happen by ensuring corrective measures were taken at the beginning of the processing stage).

The food industry standard type of inspection often included judgement-based inspections, especially at the raw material stage and finished product stage. Based on the categories, the managers should strive to minimise the dependence on the judgement-based inspections. However, inspection at the raw material stage could transform the *judgement inspection* to *source inspection*, as a way of preventing defective raw materials from being processed. The objective of inspection is to ensure only non-defective products are sold to the

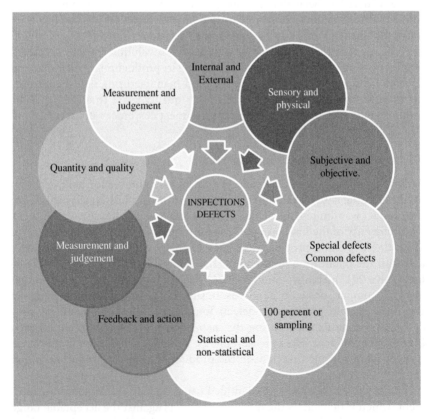

Figure 4.1 Inspection for defects.

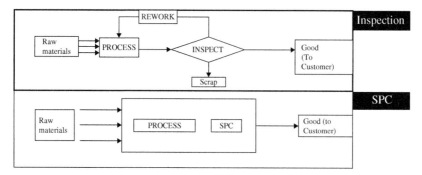

Figure 4.2 Inspection vs SPC.

customers, which it is almost similar to the SPC application. However, the differences of the mechanism from each approach displayed in Figure 4.2, sets SPC as the recommended quality control technique.

The inspection being at the end of the production line only permits manufacturers to identify the accepted products reaching the standard outlined, as well as rejected products that fail to achieve the standards. This mechanism reflected that the inspection was executed but it does not include any of the control efforts! Critical differences that opt out of inspection as a quality control technique are depicted in the Figure 4.3.

It is necessary to design the quality control system with minimal inspection as the maximal efficient inspection efforts are of little value towards

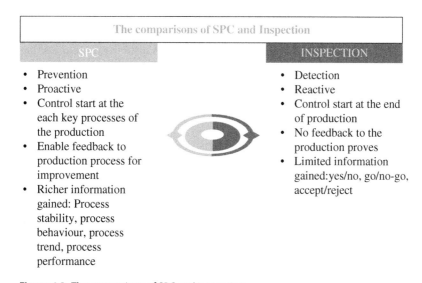

Figure 4.3 The comparison of SPC and inspection.

the operations. In fact, Deming (1986) accentuated that even if there is an inspection at each end-product produced, it does not necessarily assure quality. Both Deming (1986) and Crosby (1984) agreed on the basic policy of eliminating product defects by prevention instead of reaction.

Another reason for discouraging the usage of inspection is the approach is expensive. 100% inspection is expensive in nature since the sampling plan of the product involves all samples. Despite all samples involved in the inspection process, the effectiveness of the approach is highly doubtful. As output of an inspection involved on bad/good product, there is very little information offered to the inspector. Further question may arise; what is the level of the bad product considered bad product? Lack of details and information on the inspection output is a critical barrier to the effort to improve the process. The mechanism behind inspection failed to embrace the continuous improvement philosophy which is one of the criteria to enhance business competitive advantage.

You cannot inspect quality into a product!

(Harold F. Dodge)

4.3   The Evolution of SPC in the Food Industry

The statistical approach to quality control has its origins in the invention of the control chart by a physician Walter Andrew Shewhart for the Bell Telephone Laboratory in the 1920s. However, it was not until the late 1940s when Edwards Deming adopted Shewhart's work, found that the use of statistical techniques, such as control charting could be beneficial in the manufacturing industry. Pereira and Aspinwall (1991) reported that it was not until the mid-1950s that the use of statistical quality control (SQC) methods in the food industry became significant. One of the first successful applications was the control of container filling processes (Herschdoerfer 1967; Pereira and Aspinwall 1993). Until then, most of the SQC applications in the food industry took place in the packaging process.

A window of opportunity for improvement in the process control techniques opened when the food industry began to apply SQC method and integrated it with the operational research technique, known as the Evolutionary Operations (EVOPs). Developed by George E. P. Box in 1950, EVOP is a process optimisation technique through systematic experimentation. Compared to Design of Experiment (DOE), EVOP is applied to avoid interrupted production flow while conducting trials and experimentations.

From quality control, the concept of quality assurance spread in the food processors in 1970s, which was believed to be the best remedy for the quality issues faced by the food industry. One of the significant foci, especially in the USA,

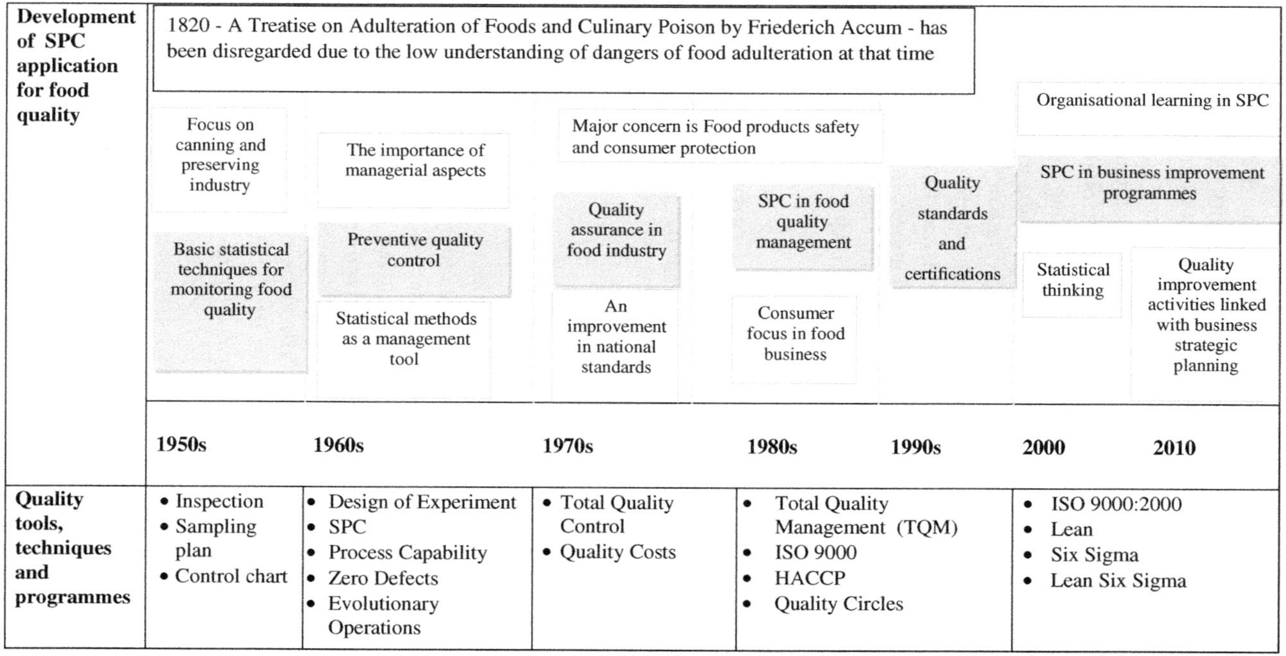

Development of SPC application for food quality	1820 - A Treatise on Adulteration of Foods and Culinary Poison by Friederich Accum - has been disregarded due to the low understanding of dangers of food adulteration at that time					
	Focus on canning and preserving industry	The importance of managerial aspects	Major concern is Food products safety and consumer protection	SPC in food quality management	Quality standards and certifications	Organisational learning in SPC
	Basic statistical techniques for monitoring food quality	Preventive quality control	Quality assurance in food industry	Consumer focus in food business		SPC in business improvement programmes
		Statistical methods as a management tool	An improvement in national standards			Statistical thinking
						Quality improvement activities linked with business strategic planning
	1950s	**1960s**	**1970s**	**1980s**	**1990s**	**2000** **2010**
Quality tools, techniques and programmes	• Inspection • Sampling plan • Control chart	• Design of Experiment • SPC • Process Capability • Zero Defects • Evolutionary Operations	• Total Quality Control • Quality Costs	• Total Quality Management (TQM) • ISO 9000 • HACCP • Quality Circles		• ISO 9000:2000 • Lean • Six Sigma • Lean Six Sigma

Figure 4.4 Evolution of SPC in the food industry.

was the establishment of the Food Products Safety and Consumer Protection Act. By achieving this, an integrated quality system was suggested, and Good Manufacturing Practice (GMP) was proposed (Hubbard 2013; van der Spiegel et al. 2003). In 1986, the American Society for Quality Control (ASQC) published the Food Processing Industry Quality Systems Guidelines outlining the basic elements of structuring and evaluating the systems required for food production. Additionally, the utilisation of SPC has facilitated Hazard Analysis Critical Control Point (HACCP) applications to control and monitor the process in real time (Grigg 1998; Hayes, Scallan, and Wong 1997).

Entering the millennium years, quality control study, especially in the food industry, has diverted its direction to nurturing a statistical thinking mindset in the business (Grigg and Walls 2007a; Hersleth and Bjerke 2001). The culture of CI and statistical thinking turn to a new perspective on the quality related issues in the food industry, where quality control and improvement activities are not only useful at the production line but also for the other business units across the organisation. Figure 4.4 maps the evolution of SPC in the food industry.

4.4   The Principle of Current Quality Control

Generally, quality control activities in the current food industry highly involve three phases, which are:

- Raw material
- Processing
- Finished product

Commonly in the food business, little can be corrected or altered after the food product has been produced or manufactured and reaches the end of the production line. Corrective action is disabled after the product is being produced and therefore it is considered too late! Therefore, quality control activities in the food industry should emphasise on the quality of raw materials and control the processes involved in manufacturing the products. On paper, it is the perfect plan, (to ensure a 100% focus on the raw material quality control and the processes used), however, in practice, it is difficult to guarantee that the company has complete control over raw materials and processing conditions.

4.4.1   Control in Raw Material

Warehouses in the food industry commonly involve a diverse range of raw materials, that have different shelf-life. For example, ingredients such as spices, flours, and colourings may be applied gradually but still have a longer shelf-life.

Some of the ingredients may rapidly be applied and required to be frequently stored, while, some are easily perishable, which requires specific continuous storage condition. However, if all the ingredients (including minor ingredients) are all to be assessed based on its condition, the cost of the inspections itself will become a disadvantage/burden instead of an advantage. The manufacturers should plan the quality control system by prioritising to monitor the main ingredients for the products continuously. The key ingredients should be selected through an establishment, related to the ingredients that may have a direct impact on the product quality. Some of the raw material quality control requires a long time for the testing process to be completed (chemical, physical, microbiological), but the raw materials should only be released from the warehouse only if the test results were known and recorded. In this industry, it is common to discuss the quality of the process control with assumptions that the raw materials are under a proper control system, and the main raw material is guaranteed to achieve the standards for quality processing.

4.4.2 Control in the Finished Product

This is one of the phases centred around the quality control activities in most of the food businesses. The assessment of the finished product typically implemented before the packaging process, only allowing the acceptance of material to comply to the quality limits (standards) and rejecting the products which failed to attain the standards. However, such a mechanism is hardly depicting quality control. Instead it is a reflection of the inspection process as little can be done to correct the product quality. In the present, emphasis is given to the process control as a critical aspect in manufacturing, depicted as an evolution of strategic thinking in the industry; from detection to prevention. Prevention is able to be achieved by improving the control system in process where it served as a diagnostic tool.

4.4.3 Control in Processing

Processing in the food industry typically involves a combination of procedures, which can be categorised as unit operations that change from raw materials to final products. The combination of several selected unit operations into unit processes is what makes up food processing. Some of the operation units may contribute significantly towards the quality of the products, whereas the unit operations should be systematically monitored and controlled.

There are many reasons why the processes in the food industry are challenging to be controlled. One of the reasons is due to the inherent variability. The natural or inherent variability is impossible to eliminate, as it is considered as a common variability that exists in any process. Although most inherent variation does not cause any major disruption to the process, it is often difficult to determine if the process needs be readjusted or if the change is a result of a natural variation process that will self-correct. Statistical techniques are one of the best approaches used to predict the situation and out-of-control variations.

Key purpose of process control programme:

- The products are consistently meeting the specifications
- Ensure only acceptable products to be produced at each step of the production process.
- Focus on maintaining the stability of the process.
- Continuous reduction in the variability in the processing and end product

An appropriate process control programme necessitates a complete understanding of the process itself. Therefore, in planning a process control scheme, it is crucial first to list the actual sequence of the processing steps and this includes the processes involving raw materials. Through the preparation of the list of steps, several processing points will be identified and marked as critical points (CPs) that have the potential risks of lowering the quality of the final products.

Usually, if the process has been established, these critical points are referred to be identified and documented. Although this may be true for some of the cases, there is a significant probability of finding the potential causes of problems as the team carefully analyses the details involved in each step, that could have been missed and provide new ideas for preventing problems. Identifying the critical points of the process does not involve the action of the control yet, as later, the points need to be systematically monitored and controlled to ensure no extreme process variations.

An effective process control system adds value and improves the common audit process, which is implemented by most of the food businesses. Typically, a comprehensive inspection is required for product-manufacturing daily audit, to ensure that the procedure reflects the actual practices, to determine the variations for efficient correction action, to implement a proactive process improvement approach and to encourage continuous corrective action efforts.

In order to avoid delay caused by inspection and testing, a strategic control of flow between warehouse control, quality control and plant management is essential.

4.4.4 The Practicality of SPC in the Food Industry

The majority of SPC application studies depicted an integration of SPC with other quality tools and techniques especially the DOE. Most of the integrated SPC-HACCP cases refer to food safety control and the main issue discussed in these cases concerns the validation of critical control points (CCPs). Although HACCP has become the most reliable and cost-effective method of food safety management due to its main principal concepts (prevention and documentation), there are still some weaknesses of HACCP. SPC is viewed to be the best solution for one of the inherent weaknesses of safety control in HACCP; there is no approach of having advanced signals to warn the potential occurrences when the CCPs exceed the critical limit zone. Hayes, Scallan, and Wong (1997) highlighted that instead of just getting Pass/Fail classification of the Relative Light Units (RLUs) of the rapid hygiene testing systems, SPC enables a food company to obtain an advanced warning on the status of critical point (CP).

Commonly after the HACCP plan was adequately validated and implemented in the food businesses, the team may assume that the most challenging process has ended. However, this is just the beginning of the hard task! The primary challenge of its implementation is to sustain effective HACCP application during day-to-day operations. In order to improve its effectiveness and to keep safety parameters in control, a systematic process control technology should be integrated into HACCP steps.

Example 4.1

Commodity	Applications	Advantages
Eggs	There is no evidence of the effectiveness of HACCP elements in controlling the eggs from the safety hazards.	The CCP value validated (All control measures are capable of being designed with critical limits except chlorine level).
Meat processing and preserving	The low rate of unsatisfactory batches of *Enterobacteriaceae* and *Pseudomonas* count detection caused doubt on the efficiency of the traditional control scheme.	Validates the assumption of microbiological contamination variances is in control (2% variances above the control limit).
Meat processing and preserving Dalgiç, Vardin, and BelibaÄŸli (2011)	There is demand for more effective quality control technique to assist HACCP implementation.	Stabilise the moisture content (reading approximately 40%). Able to prioritise five critical problems. Enable plant operators to take action quickly. • 3 months

Commodity	Applications	Advantages
Dairy Hayes, Scallan, and Wong (1997)	There is neither proper trend analysis nor warning to out-of-control CP in the RLU – reading for adenosine triphosphate (ATP) Bioluminescence Technique for food safety purposes.	Provide warning in FAIL case as early as Day 51 before the out-of-control on Day 74. Depict better prevention, control system with the integration of SPC and HACCP • 3 months
Nut Hurst and Harris (2013)	SPC is applied to avoid unsafe nuts product, Salmonella and *Escherichia coli* contamination, which caused manufacturers to establish a HACCP-like safety plan.	The air temperature should be able to be continuously adjusted in order to avoid microbial contamination.

Applications of SPC involves several critical parameters identified in the food processes. These appertain sensory attributes (i.e. size, weight, texture, colour, height) and safety attributes (i.e. microbial counts). In the same way, for the food industry, SPC implementation's prime characteristics of quality include food safety attributes, sensory attributes and packaging attributes of the products. It was reported in the seminar of quality control for processed food by the Asian Productivity Organization (APO) that a Japanese food quality pre-requisite programme named *Importance of the Quality Control,* where they highlighted the most important criteria in quality control of processed food to be safety and reliability, followed by 'deliciousness' and 'appropriate price' (Raju 2005).

Example 4.2

Commodity	Applications	Advantages
Bakery Hung and Sung (2011)	X-bar and R-chart applied during re-steaming bun process, customers' complaints that the product has issues such as shrinkage, foreign material and crack.	Decrease the 70% shrinkage rate (defects).

Commodity	Applications	Advantages
Biscuits (Srikaeo, Furst, and Ashton 2005)	Best practice is required for process characterisation either for new process or for when a process has undergone significant engineering change.	Able to detect the worst line performance; Cpk 0.63 < 1.33 (required values). An inadequate measurement system with operators' measurement variations for wheat protein and moisture content contributes 92.21% and 98.84% of total variation respectively.
Nuts Özdemir and Özilgen (1997)	Production of hazelnuts worth £312 480 500 faced a quality problem of damage during the cracking process.	The quality performance is clear and able to detect the need for equipment readjustment and the operational problem (crusher equipment).
Tea Rai (2008)	Cumulative Sum (CUSUM) chart applied to overcome the critical problem faced in tea production is the weight variation in the tea packet (underweight or overweight).	Reduction of out-of-control situation from 66% to 4%
Confectionary Knowles, Johnson, and Warwood (2004)	X-bar chart applied to reduce the variation in the sweet size caused reworks, scraps, machine downtime.	The air temperature able to be continuously fixed and avoid the microbial contamination.

4.5 Future of SPC: Organisational Learning Through Statistical Methods Application

Following the principals of statistical thinking (explained in Chapter 1), the statistical methods applied in quality improvement efforts, involved systematic assessments of variations in processes using the quality set of data. Three principal attributes which contribute to developing learning efficiency of humans are skills, knowledge, and attributes (SKAs) (Stamatis 2002). Then, this is facilitated by the critical activities for building learning organisation, which are systematic problem solving, trials and experimentation, continuous learning from experiences, transferring knowledge, and objectively assessing the learning process. The principal attributes and critical activities of building the learning organisation are found to be reflected by the SPC implementation process. For example, along the implementation of SPC, the process data were captured, stored, analysed and interpreted, and linked with the performance measures. This data may then be filed as records; whereby some of the identified critical issues raised from the data will be discussed with the team for process improvement purposes.

Organisational learning (OL) is accredited to the action learning process in which Argyris and Schön (1978) postulated that there is dual structure of OL. OL is defined as the process of organisational change that modifies their mental models, processes, knowledge, rules, maintaining or improving their performances (Argyris and Schön 1978; Senge 2014).

Learning starts with experience and there are dimensions of experience proposed by Argote and Miron-Spektor (2011), including direct and indirect experience (refer Figure 4.5). The understanding of learning experience depends on the identification of the source of learning activities in transforming experience towards knowledge.

Within the context of SPC implementation, learning is regarded as the centre of the CI activities of existing processes and the discovery of novel processes. Learning such activities ensures mistakes are not repeated and more importantly, that it was applied in the existing processes. Such foundation of knowledge in organisational systems, encourages CI (Locke and Jain 1995). Past studies in OL relevant to operations improvement may be grouped into several general categories (see Figure 4.6).

Interest towards the OL has risen due to the increasingly unstable environment in which organisations operate (Lee 2000). Organisations were required to increase their ability to learn due to the restructuring of industries and the impact of information technology. The creation of learning and knowledge are claimed to be related to *how* the organisation manages the cognitive processes of its members (Choo, Linderman, and Schroeder 2007). Typically, learning opportunities in the food companies are related to the activities in the training department (Grigg 2007b; Hersleth 2001), which profoundly concerns individuals' skills and knowledge (Hewson 1996; Gaspar 2015; Cheng 1998). The act of merely treating a training session as peripheral and at times easily neglected, facilitating learning throughout the organisations currently become critical components facilitating organisational change. The world of industries is changing where different approaches of learning which encompasses the whole organisation, is required (Lee, Bennett, and Oakes 2000). One of the objectives of this research is to understand the type of learning that occurs in an organisation within the implementation of SPC explained by the OL theory where Argyris and Schön (1978) postulated a *single-loop learning* and *double-loop learning* model:

- *Single-loop learning.* Corporate that achieve their goal or correct an error without re-assessing their underlying values may be said to be practising

Learning from direct experience

- Learning can generally involve practicing through events that are incremental in nature (Argote & Miron-Spektor, 2011; Upton & Kim, 1998).
- Foundation of direct experience learning was based on direct observation on self- practices for process performance improvement.
- It can be iterative and organisations commonly "choose from a pool of alternative routines, adopting better ones when they are discovered" and/or "trial-and-error experimentations" (Locke & Jain, 1995).
- Examples: initiatives in CI such as the DOE, Taguchi method, evolutionary operation, and *kaizen*.
- Practice-based theories of learning: Learning can exists in "communities-of-practice" and workgroups, not necessarily formulated by the company, which emerged at the workplace. Such workgroups gain knowledge through enculturation (learn from other members of the community)

Learning from indirect experience

- Involves a range of observational activities of others to gain knowledge from outside of the company, and subsequently applying the knowledge to improve its processes and performance (Argote, 2013).
- Sources: government agencies, professional bodies, published information, transfer of employees from different department, training sessions, consultants, benchmarking, and strategic treaties to support this type of learning.
- The publicised successful problem-solving effort will encourage people to recognise and be aware of the potential benefits of engaging in quality improvement activities (Tucker, Edmondson, & Spear, 2002).
- The organisational units can practice learning activities from other business units, which is also known as knowledge transfer.

Figure 4.5 Learning through experience.

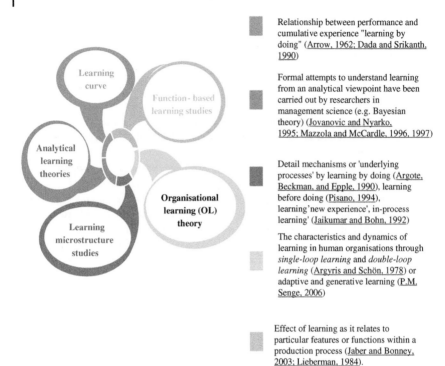

Relationship between performance and cumulative experience "learning by doing" (Arrow, 1962; Dada and Srikanth, 1990)

Formal attempts to understand learning from an analytical viewpoint have been carried out by researchers in management science (e.g. Bayesian theory) (Jovanovic and Nyarko, 1995; Mazzola and McCardle, 1996, 1997)

Detail mechanisms or 'underlying processes' by learning by doing (Argote, Beckman, and Epple, 1990), learning before doing (Pisano, 1994), learning 'new experience', in-process learning' (Jaikumar and Bohn, 1992)

The characteristics and dynamics of learning in human organisations through *single-loop learning* and *double-loop learning* (Argyris and Schön, 1978) or adaptive and generative learning (P.M. Senge, 2006)

Effect of learning as it relates to particular features or functions within a production process (Jaber and Bonney, 2003; Lieberman, 1984).

Figure 4.6 Relation of OL in process improvement.

the *single-loop learning* strategy *(*Argyris 1995). According to Krüger (1999) from the quality perspective, learning model relates to inspection approach, 'fire-fighting' and troubleshooting activities. Operators are alerted to an occurring problem, and corrective action is taken to bring the process back into control. Such approaches provide limited opportunity to learn from the experience of fixing the problem and leading to shallow understanding (Murray and Chapman 2003). Besides that, it will also not necessarily prevent future recurrence of the problem (Upton and Kim 1998). This is due to the level of learning as *single-loop learning* focuses on solving problems without any examination of the appropriateness of organisational practices that induced the problem. *Single-loop learning* is also based on short-term rationality and immediate purpose. Therefore, *single-loop learning* occurs more frequently and incrementally (Upton and Kim 1998). According to William et al. (1989), larger and stable organisations depend significantly on *single-loop learning* that is following the existing rules (i.e. bureaucracy).

- *Double loop learning. Double-loop learning* focuses on questioning why the errors or successes occurred that it modified an organisation's implicit norms and objectives (Buckler 1996; Marquardt 1996). In quality management perspectives, *double-loop learning* corresponds to modifying the process (altering principal variables within the system) to understand and eliminate the causes of problems, prevent recurrence of problems and foster CI (Argyris 1995; Gijo 2005). According to Argyris (1995) and Blackman et al. (2004), *double-loop learning* is a necessity to occur for focusing on sustainable change (implementation of SPC) in an organisation. Fine (1986, 1988) stated that ignoring the learning potential of quality control activities may lead to under-investment in quality improvement activities and subsequently hinder quality competitiveness. Murray and Chapman (2003) claimed from their empirical studies that quality control under TQM is most successful when improvements are embodied in *double-loop learning* routine as a continuous learning journey.

Quality control is viewed as a task involving *single-loop learning* as it makes sure the processes are running in compliance with the standards and regulations (Tucker, Edmondson, and Spear 2002). Similar to the claims by Grigg (2007a,b), most of SPC efforts are viewed as a single-loop learning practices. The current state of quality initiatives implementation are effective in the existing technology and current customer needs, however, it was viewed less effective in exploring the new technologies and understanding emerging customer needs (Choo, Linderman, and Schroeder 2007). However, according to Ogland (2014), quality improvement activities with the involvement to improving the standards and procedures in an organisation contributed to *double-loop learning*. The usage of a structured problem-solving approach in Six Sigma with the applications of other quality techniques for variance reduction method suggests the strong orientation towards exploratory learning (Choo, Linderman, and Schroeder 2007). In light of the process and effort to adopt SPC as a new technology in the food companies, *double-loop learning* is required to take place for the change to be a success (Lee 2000).

During the process of implementing new operation management technology (e.g. SPC) in the business, individuals and the organisation's system and practices would undergo some transformation, which requires shifts in the employees' thinking and behaviour (Rusly, Corner, and Sun 2012). Through the application of SPC, the organisations may start to question about the target they set for themselves and how they are trying to achieve these targets, which may involve *second-loop learning* characteristics (Jeliazkova and Westerheijden 2002).

The procedure of CI implementation process seems to catalyse learning and push CI forward (Buckler 1996; Savolainen and Haikonen 2007), but it does not mean *double-loop* learning is achievable (Argyris and Schön 1978). Identifying and managing both types of learning is beneficial for the long-term development of SPC potential, since at diverse stages there will be a need for reinforcing *single-loop learning* and system change (*double-loop learning*) (Bessant and

Francis 1999; Choo, Linderman, and Schroeder 2007; Grigg and Walls 2007b). *Double-loop learning* is the hallmark of a learning organisation, and is imperative for converting individual and team learning into a learning organisation (Buckler 1996).

Although several studies have explored the underlying concept of OL and learning curve activities, the majority fall short of informing managers on the activities supporting OL for lasting process improvement (Upton and Kim 1998). Savolainen and Haikonen (2007) highlighted that the effective application of quality methods requires appropriate OL strategies. Based on the context of SPC, continuous improvement is based on learning. Normally, how the process of OL through SPC is viewed can be executed through converting data to information resulting from the relevant statistical analysis (Grigg and Walls 2007b). Sustaining the quality advantage is the critical impact from the consideration of learning and knowledge creation in CI initiatives for quality (Choo, Linderman, and Schroeder 2007).

4.6 Summary

- SPC is defined and viewed beyond as a process monitoring technique within continuous improvement efforts.
- Variation is the foci of SPC implementation
- The objective of SPC is process stability through variation reduction.
- Quality control activities in the food industry involve raw material control, process control and finished product quality control.
- Before SPC, inspection is the only quality control effort where it is the first approach to separating the defects from the good products before they arrive for customers.
- Inspection should be minimalised as prevention is preferable to reaction approach.
- The implementation of other techniques with SPC strengthens SPC application as the previous evidence shows that besides significant reduction of process variations, food safety control can be improved (e.g. integration of SPC and HACCP).
- SPC activities may contribute to the organisation learning culture in the organisation.

5

Tools in SPC

5.1   Basic Quality Tools

Controlling the process is not just about constructing and applying control charts. It is an activity that should become part of the primary business strategy in the services industry. In order to maintain the consistency of a process or to reduce the variability in production, problem-solving activities commonly need to take place. Problem-solving activities are not particularly new to quality management in the food industry. In fact, problem-solving efforts are commonly facilitated by the usage of a variety of quality tools. Quality tools have a long history – some of the tools were even applied before World War II. Quality tools consist of both qualitative and quantitative approaches, which focus on improving companywide activities.

5.2   SPC Tools

Based on the Statistical Process Control (SPC) definitions discussed in the previous section, it is assumed that the tools related to SPC are broad enough to include all techniques including statistics, as well as being applicable in experiments that range from a random sample to the very sophisticated technique design of experiments (Montgomery 2012). There is no standard set of tools within SPC; however, there is a general agreement on seven tools: histograms, Pareto charts, cause-and-effect analysis (CEA)/fishbone diagrams, scatter diagrams, check sheets, and control charts. Nevertheless, it is agreed that a control chart is a primary tool within SPC. This chapter describes SPC tools and some examples of food industry application.

SPC is arguably involved with managerial issues more than mathematical literacy issues. The term 'SPC implementation' requires a clear understanding of the procedures to be adopted and activities to be performed using a set of tools, which indicate employees' participatory management. Therefore, such an argument is seconded by the implications from the dual concepts of SPC – 'the

Statistical Process Control for the Food Industry: A Guide for Practitioners and Managers, First Edition.
Sarina Abdul Halim Lim and Jiju Antony.
© 2019 John Wiley & Sons Ltd. Published 2019 by John Wiley & Sons Ltd.

operation of statistical control' and 'the state of statistical control' – suggested by Shewhart (1939). Several quality tools are applicable in more than one stage, and each tends to be particularly useful for specific tasks and objectives. The tool will be described using 4W 1H as follows:

- What is the tool?
- Why apply the tool?
- How to apply the tool?
- When to apply the tool?
- Where to apply the tool?

5.3   Cause-and-Effect Analysis

5.3.1   What?

In the food industry, the effect of the process is always known, but the cause is often unknown. A brainstorming approach is applied to identify the causes of the problem – the list is not sufficiently analysed and categorised. A cause-effect diagram is a graphical tool that demonstrates all possible causes that could lead to a particular effect, the relationships between those causes and among them, and the effect itself. The effect is most frequently a problem. However, the CEA can also be used to study the causes of a positive effect. The cause-effect diagram is also described as a 'fishbone' diagram, due to its shape resembling a fishbone, or an Ishikawa diagram (named after its inventor, Professor Kauru Ishikawa, who developed it in the 1960s). It consists of five or six categories of the following skeleton (machines, methods, materials, manpower, measurements, environments) (refer Figure 5.1).

5.3.2   Why?

To identify possible causes of the problem, uncover bottlenecks in the processes and identify where and why the process is working.

5.3.3   When?

Brainstorming session to investigate the root of a problem.

5.3.4   How?

Determine the areas that could be potential problems and allow for comparison of their relative importance. CEA is commonly constructed through brainstorming procedures. The fish-shaped diagram is formed from the causes that can result in undesirable issues/problems. A narrowed and focused premise will

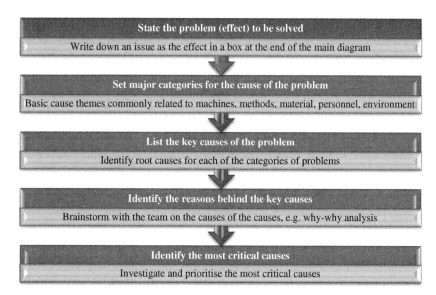

Figure 5.1 Steps to apply cause-effect analysis.

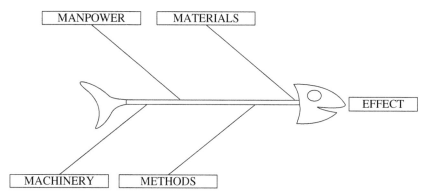

Figure 5.2 Fishbone diagram.

result in a more directed analysis of the identified causes. Figure 5.2 provide the steps to implement the CEA.

The causes are the independent variables, and the failure mode is the dependent variable (the factor at the mouth of the fish). The classification of the main possible causes will typically take the form of the classic 4Ms: manpower, methods, machines and materials. However, at this stage the classification is not ultimate, as different companies could adopt different categories depending on the situation and issues. However, it is highly suggested to use the conventional initial stage of CEA, as it happens to satisfy a lot of other cases and, if it is needed, provide a basis for further adaptation. An approach to carrying out the activity can be executed while following cause classification, process steps, and cause listing (Barone and Franco 2012). Regardless of the approaches taken for these sessions, the determination of all possible root causes is an activity to be brainstormed by a group of people that have strong awareness, great interest and profound knowledge in the effect being studied. At each stage the causes, which influence the main cause, are considered and then each of these sub-causes, in turn, is analysed, and so forth.

Discussions of the following sub-causes will occasionally be discussed outside of the brainstorming session; at this stage, the facilitator experience is vital, and the identification of the sub-causes is successful. As the diagram is developed through investigations, interviews, brainstorming sessions and 5-why questioning, the inputs become the causes of that effect, and their causes, and so on (Figure 5.3).

Common mistakes

- Providing never-ending possible causes of the problem
- Inexperienced facilitator.
- Trying to implement corrective action based on the early/initial results of cause–effect analysis.

Example 5.1 *Coconut Cake – Issues In The Cake Production*

All of the manufacturing companies that have been subcontracted from Retailer A are given specifications on their products following the consumers' preference on the products. Variation in producing the product has caused the products are not conforming to the specifications, which caused the cakes are then considered as defects and sold for animal feed. The manufacturer is facing the risk of losing financially and the contract with the Retailer A.

Purpose

The purpose of this study is to assess the causes and reasons for the defects of the cake at the production phase. However, the initial stage requires investigation of the causes that affected at each of the potential critical category and later why-why analysis was done. One of the issues identified is the recipe of the product may cause the variance of product quality.

5.3.5 Where?

- Product and process design
- Product and process improvement
- Process optimisation

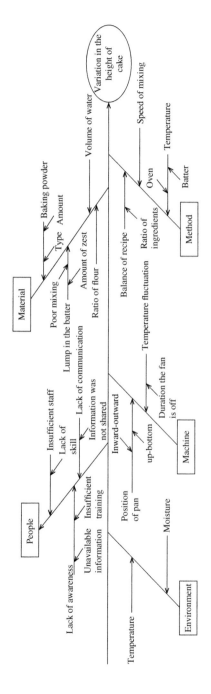

Figure 5.3 Cause-and-effect analysis for variability in the height of coconut cake production.

- Hazard and risk assessment
- Process control
- Audit (laboratory control and process, product and field performance)

5.4 Pareto Diagram

5.4.1 What?

Pareto analysis, which was developed by an Italian socialist, Alfredo Pareto, is applied to differentiate the relatively few factors which contributed to the majority of the effects. The concept of the Pareto principle is that 80% of the problems come from 20% of the factors. The idea is that, instead of focusing on the trivial matters, management should focus on the 20% of important factors that are causing major problems. The term '80/20' was first defined by Juran and is related to the Pareto principle. It is commonly applied as a rule of thumb, not developed from theoretical derivation, but accepted in practice.

A Pareto diagram looks similar to a bar chart in which all of the relevant factors contributing to an overall effect are arranged in descending order according to the magnitude of their effect. This arranged order ensures separating the 'vital few' (most critical factors) from the 'useful many' factors or inputs that are useful to understand but contributed to a relatively smaller consequence to the problems or issues. Using a Pareto diagram helps a team concentrate its efforts on the factors or inputs that have the greatest impact on the 'process to be improved' outcomes. It also helps a team communicate the rationale for focusing on certain points of the processes.

5.4.2 Why?

Pareto analysis is a method applied for prioritising problems based on the ones that occur most often. The advantage of Pareto analysis is that it can assist in straightening out the priorities with the most important areas first. This tool is effective in avoiding confusion with the initial ideas of major problems and in directly fixing those which may not be big problems. This tool helps to create a focus on the correct problems to be resolved. Common situations for the application of Pareto analysis are:

- Making sense of the data related to the frequency of causes, issues or problems in a process.
- Focusing on the most significant cause when there are many identified causes.
- Analysing broad causes by focusing on their specific components.

5.4.3 When?

After brainstorm on potential causes of the problems, prioritisation of the factors is needed as information on how critical the a factor compared to each other is unknown.

5.4.4 How?

Figure 5.4 provides the steps to develop the diagram.

Pareto analysis can be used in three situations. The most common and basic application is to identify the vital few from the trivial many for most quality systems. The other applications are comparative Pareto analysis and weighted Pareto analysis, the former of which focus on any number of options or actions (Frigon and Mathews 1997). The latter type, weighted Pareto analysis, not only identifies the frequencies of the occurrences but also estimates a measure of their importance and accounts for the severity of the defects or costs.

Example 5.2 *Potato Chips – Critical Control Points (Varzakas and Arvanitoyannis 2007)*

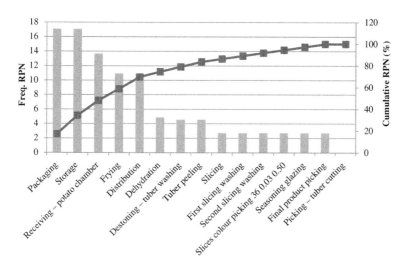

Packaging, storage, potato receiving, frying and distribution were the processes identified as having the highest RPN (Risk Priority Number) (225, 225, 180, 144 and 144, respectively) for corrective action to be implemented.

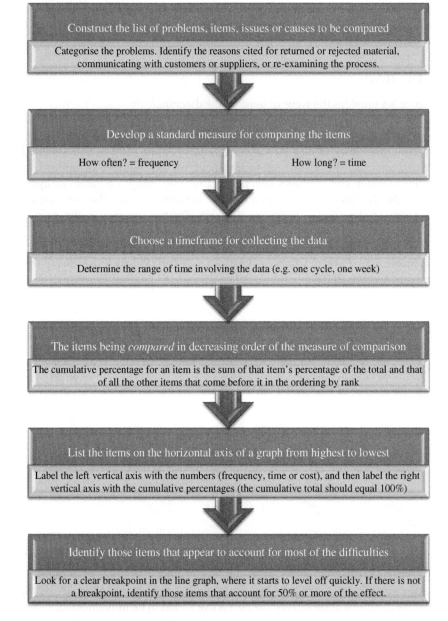

Figure 5.4 Steps to develop Pareto diagram.

5.4.5   Where?

- Customer/consumer complaint analysis
- Sensory evaluation
- Vendor selection
- Ingredient/raw material risk assessment
- Marketing and sales
- Manufacturing deficits
- Process and quality control
- Equipment maintenance priorities

5.5   Process Flowchart

5.5.1   What?

A process flowchart is a quality tool that can be applied to understand how the process is done. It is typically presented using a diagrammatic technique – it may have many paths along the way (from the start to the end of the diagram). The process flowchart can describe any process, such as a manufacturing process, an administrative or service process, and a project plan. It is a generic tool that can be adapted for a wide variety of purposes. A team can apply a process flowchart by breaking the flowchart into logical steps and identify areas that need corrective action/any potential areas causing problems to strategise the preventive action. However, a large process can result in a very complicated and confusing flowchart; therefore, breaking the process into smaller processes is the best approach.

5.5.2   Why?

A process flowchart is typically used at the beginning of a process improvement event to describe process events, timing and frequencies at the highest level and work downward. At high levels, process flowcharts facilitate managers and teams in understanding process complications. At lower levels, this quality tool helps you analyse and improve the process. In order to have better communication to explain a particular process, the usage of a process flowchart is proven effective.

In constructing the diagram of the process flowchart, some common symbols were applied in the flowchart, as listed below (Table 5.1):

5.5.3   How?

Figure 5.5 provide the steps to map the process flowchart.

Table 5.1 The common symbols used in the flowchart.

Symbols	Details	Symbols	Details
 →	Direction of the flow	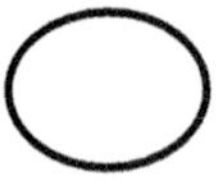 ◯	Link to another page or flowchart
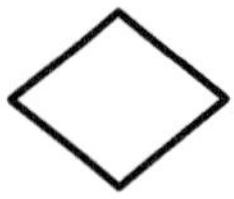 ◇	Decision	▱	Input/output
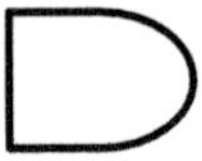 ⊃	Delay	 ▭◯	Start and end points

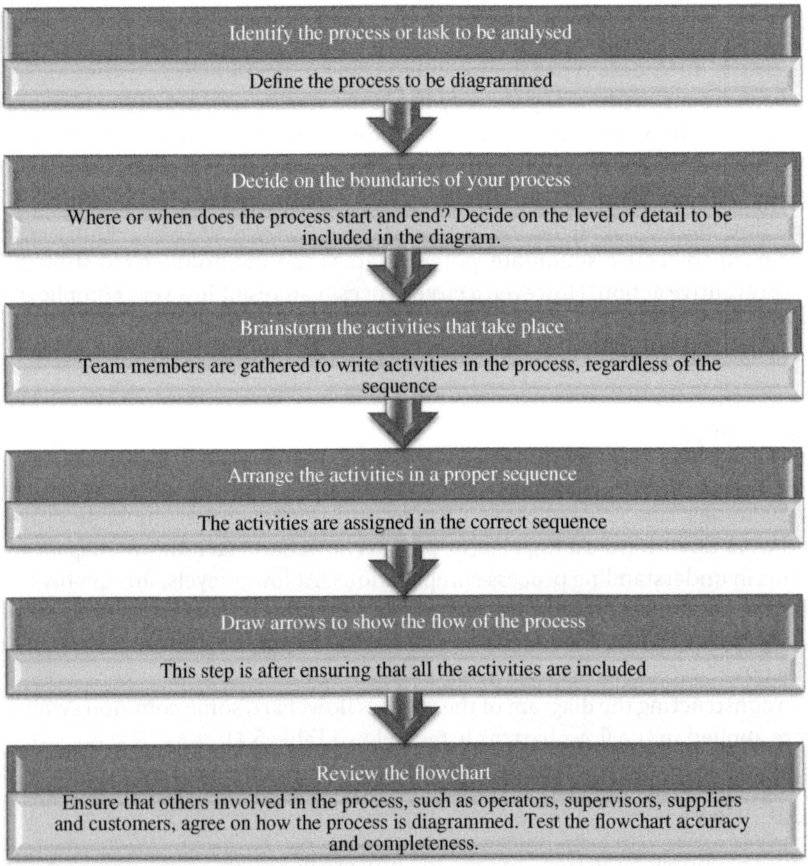

Identify the process or task to be analysed

Define the process to be diagrammed

Decide on the boundaries of your process

Where or when does the process start and end? Decide on the level of detail to be included in the diagram.

Brainstorm the activities that take place

Team members are gathered to write activities in the process, regardless of the sequence

Arrange the activities in a proper sequence

The activities are assigned in the correct sequence

Draw arrows to show the flow of the process

This step is after ensuring that all the activities are included

Review the flowchart

Ensure that others involved in the process, such as operators, supervisors, suppliers and customers, agree on how the process is diagrammed. Test the flowchart accuracy and completeness.

Figure 5.5 Steps to develop process flowchart.

5.5.4 When?

It is imperative for the team to understand the steps and details of the process. In order to identify key processes and critical quality parameters to control, drawing process flowchart is a big help.

Example 5.3 *Sweets (Knowles, Johnson, and Warwood 2004)*
A team is improving medicated sweet manufacturing processes – the team mapped the process using the affinity approach, with all of the team members being allowed to generate their version of events. The team then discussed and refined the ideas to form one process that was agreed by all.

Simple flowchart

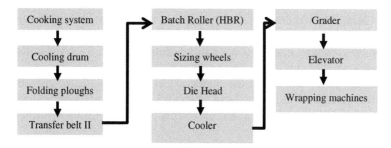

The agreed process flowchart is shown in above figure and formed the basis of future discussions.

5.5.5 Where?

- Process control and monitoring
- Process improvement
- Process characterisation

5.6 Histogram

5.6.1 What?

A histogram is one of the simplest graphical tools typically applied to visualise variation and display the distribution of a process. Compared to stem and leaf analysis, a histogram facilitates managers in visualising patterns and trends in data variation which are not readily apparent in table forms, especially the shape of data distribution. The histogram was first implemented by Kaoru Ishikawa, one of the Japanese quality gurus.

5.6.2 Why?

The primary purpose of using a histogram is to see this shape of data distribution, analysing the dispersion of the data and finding the peak of the data. Typically, a histogram is used to find and characterise the distribution of data after prioritisation has been implemented through Pareto analysis.

5.6.3 When?

The team to identify the distribution of the data.

5.6.4 How?

The construction of a histogram can be done manually or use software, although it is slightly tedious and error-prone when done manually. Software such as Excel, Minitab and Statistical Package for the Social Sciences (SPSS) are readily available and easy to use for this purpose. Figure 5.6 provide the steps to develop histogram.

The potential interpretation of the histogram provides the team with the shape of the variation in the data. From there, it can construct a hypothesis related to why the process data are exhibiting such trends of variation.

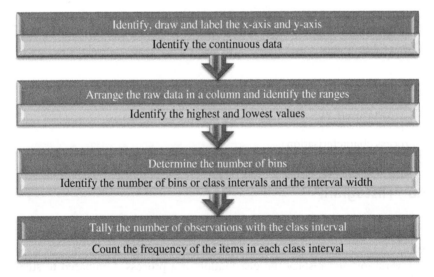

Figure 5.6 Steps to develop histogram.

Distributions of the data may follow a bell shape, skewed shape, truncated shape, isolated peak, comb shape, bi-modal shape, and plateau shape.

5.6.5 Where?

- Stock and storage distribution analysis
- Estimation of the maintenance workload
- Process characterisation
- Customer/consumer complaint analysis
- Process performance distribution
- Analysis of shifts in downtime distribution
- Raw material supplier reliability
- Microbiology testing analysis

5.7 Scatter Diagram

5.7.1 What?

A scatter diagram is a type of graph that has similar features to a line graph, except that there are points plotted without the connecting line drawn between them. It is also known as a scatter plot, which has at least two major objects that are needed for the quarries (x-axis and y-axis). The diagram cannot be used to assess a causal relationship; however, it indicates the strength of the relationship and proves the existence of it.

5.7.2 Why?

The main purpose is to reflect on what will happen to the factor and then the other effect, the change. It is also used as a graphical depiction of regression analysis and a reflection of causes and effects explained in a fishbone diagram. The slope of the diagram contained information on the type of relationship that exists between the variables. A scatter diagram also provides a visual comparison of the numbers from the tally sheet.

5.7.3 When?

To show how strong the correlation of two variables? It is particularly useful in identifying potential root causes of problems.

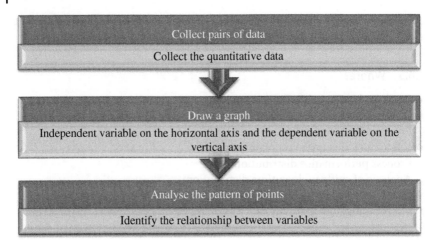

Figure 5.7 Steps to plot scatter diagram.

5.7.4 How?

Figure 5.7 provide the steps to plot and develop the diagram.

5.7.5 Where?

- Product and process improvement
- Process control
- Process and product design
- Downtime trend
- Trend of craft productivity

5.8 Control Chart

5.8.1 What?

A control chart is one of the most technically sophisticated tools of SPC, and it is considered the core tool of the technique. It was invented by Dr. Walter A. Shewhart of the Bell Telephone Labs in the 1920s as an approach to the solution to the manufacturing process variation problem to improve the economic and efficiency of the process.

A control chart is a graphical display of the critical quality parameters that have been measured typically through a range of time, and the usage of the control chart is suggested to be in a continuous manner. A control chart contains three lines – the two highest and lowest lines are known as control limits:

- The centreline represents the average value of the measured parameters.
- The upper-limit line represents the highest value of the acceptable quality standards of the product.
- The lower-limit line represents the lowest value of the acceptable quality standards of the product.

5.8.2 How?

The mechanism of clarifying a process in the state in the control is by ensuring that all the sample points fall between the control limits, indicating that there is no further corrective action required. However, if the point falls outside of the control limits, the process is interpreted as out of control or in an out-of-control state, indicating that investigations, feedback plans and corrective action are required.

The control chart is testing the proposition that the data of the process/product are consistent and uniform and that variation is caused by normal or inherent causes. If the hypothesis is rejected, special, or unusual, causes of error are assumed to be present, requiring further investigation of the root of the causes and implementation of corrective action.

In manufacturing sites, processes will commonly operate in actual consistency for a relatively long period. However, the stability of the process does not permanently last long, as at one point there will be a process shift, with an out-of-control situation causing variation in end-product quality parameters. Therefore, close process monitoring is important in identifying the art of the conscious state of the process when the process output does not conform to the range of outlined standards.

5.8.3 Assumptions

Control charts are constructed based on the assumptions that the process data are normally distributed, and the observed characteristic is distributing independently where there is no autocorrelation in the process.

5.8.4 Why?

5.8.4.1 Process/Product Monitoring

A control chart is applied to reflect the process performance as an online process monitoring technique and, subsequently, facilitate managers in deciding whether the process should be investigated for further process improvement activities. In order to avoid any nonconforming products manufactured, corrective action will be taking place after the control chart detects the occurrence of assignable causes of process shifts. Although a control chart can be applied using historical data, the primary purpose of a control chart is to prevent defective items from being produced.

Most experts recommend that a process should not be changed unless there is statistical evidence showing the process in that condition. However, it does not indicate that the process should not be improved at all, as the improvement can be implemented not by tampering with the process, but by changing the design of the process. A control chart ensures process stability as a pre-requirement before continuous improvement team members change the process design or tamper with the process settings.

5.8.4.2 Process Prediction

Another function of a control chart is to facilitate the determination of process capability by estimating the parameters of the selected process. Process prediction can be identified by using a run chart or control chart, as both have the capability of reflecting the trend of the process. However, a run chart is incapable of predicting if the process is going to be out of control over time, as it does not apply any control limits. The disadvantages of a run chart highlighted the importance of a control chart as the alternative for process prediction, provided the process is conforming to the assumptions.

5.8.5 How?

Although the most renowned control charts implemented in the food industry are Shewhart charts, the table above shows that there are many types of control charts formulated to improve the applicability of control charts in a variety of process environments. There are different ways in which to construct each of the control charts, but the common steps for the construction of a control chart can be illustrated in Figure 5.8

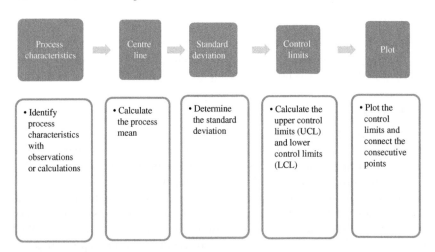

Figure 5.8 Steps to construct control charts.

5.8.6   Types of Control Charts

There are several types of control charts, and a correct control chart selection is a critical part of creating a control chart. If the wrong control chart is selected, the control limits will not be correct for the collected data. To choose the type of control chart to be used is determined by the types of data to be plotted and the format in that these data have been collected.

5.8.7   Variable Control Chart

Variable control charts are fitting for the use of continuous data or data that can be measured. Most food manufacturing process parameters measured use these types of data. The most typically applied variable control charts are the individual and moving-range (I-MR) chart, Xbar and R chart, and Xbar and S chart.

Once the data is identified to be continuous, an appropriate chart is to be chosen. The question is how to choose the appropriate chart. At this point, it will be heavily influenced by the size of the subgroup. The tips for choosing a suitable chart are as follows: if the subgroup size is 1, the type of control chart suitable to be applied is the I-MR chart; if the subgroup size ranges from 2 to 10, the Xbar chart and R chart should be applied; and if the subgroup size is more than or equal to 11, the Xbar chart and S chart are appropriate to be applied.

5.8.7.1   Xbar Chart and R Chart or Xbar and S Chart

The Xbar and R charts are SPC charts for the use of variable data collected at set time intervals in subgroups – usually between three and five samples in each subgroup. The two charts are designed to be interpreted in a paired manner. The top graph charted is the mean of each subgroup (Xbar) and the bottom graph charted is the range (R) of the subgroup.

Which type of chart to begin?

Commonly, we will begin with the Xbar-S chart in order to understand the stability of the process parameters. However, if the sample size is relatively small, then the Xbar-R chart should be the alternative option.

However, the issue with the Xbar-R chart is that as the subgroup size increases, the range used to measure within-group variation becomes poorer. Therefore, the Xbar-S chart is the solution to the problem when the subgroup size increases and becomes larger.

Out-of-control points or patterns can be detected on either the Xbar or R chart or on both charts. This is one of the most commonly encountered types of control chart, and leverages two different observations:

- The Xbar chart: how much variation exists in the process over time
- The R chart: variation within each variable (subgroups)

Prior to the wide usage of software and technology, practitioners in the food industry are reluctant to apply the Xbar-S chart instead of the Xbar-R chart. The biggest blockage of the use of the Xbar-S chart is that the concept of standard deviation is just not as easy to understand as the range. Although the Xbar-S chart is very similar to the Xbar-R chart, the key difference is that the subgroup standard deviation is plotted when using the Xbar-S chart, while the subgroup range is plotted when using the Xbar-R chart. One benefit of applying standard deviation compared to the range is that the standard deviation calculation considers all of the data points, not just the maximum and the minimum values of the data. Therefore, standard deviation depicts a better estimate of the variation in large subgroups than does the range.

Shewhart's control chart has shortages such as:

- Only consider the information in the last sample observation, ignoring information in the entire sequence of points
- Being relatively insensitive to small process shifts
- Being less useful in phase II

5.8.7.2 Exponentially Weighted Moving Average (EWMA) Chart

S.W. Roberts first introduced the exponentially weighted moving average (EWMA) control chart in 1959, followed by Wortham and Ringer (1971). They proposed that the EWMA chart is appropriate for usage in the process and manufacturing industries and financial and management control systems, in which subgroups are not practical.

Similar to CUSUM, it has the advantage of detecting small shifts in the process mean. They are especially appropriate for individuals' charts, where they can make up for the small subgroup size effectively. Unlike the Shewhart charts, single observations are usually used for this type of chart. The measurements of observations may be averages (when the individual readings making up the average are not available), individual observations' data points, ratios, proportions, or similar measurements. When designing an EWMA chart it is essential to consider the average run length and shift to be detected.

- The limits for warning and action of the EWMA chart differ from those of a Shewhart chart and have to be computed separately.

Although EWMA is widely applied to forecasting time series as well, it is not as popular as Shewhart charts. The significant difference between EWMA and the CUSUM chart is that it is using the additional weighting factor, which enables the adjustment of shift sensitivity. Although both CUSUM and EWMA charts are sensitive to small shifts in the process mean, they do not have a similar ability to a Shewhart chart in detecting larger shifts. Therefore, these two charts were sometimes applied by pairing up with a Shewhart chart (Montgomery 2012). Further extensive guidance is available in Montgomery (2012).

5.8.7.3 Cumulative Sum (CUSUM) Chart

Cumulative sum (CUSUM) control charts were first proposed by Page (1954) and had been studied by many authors; in particular, see Ewan (1963), Page (1961), Gan (1991), Lucas (1976), Hawkins (1981, 1993), and Woodall and Adams (1993). The construction of a CUSUM chart involves plotting the CUSUMs of the deviations of the sample values from a target value. Instead of assessing the subgroup mean independently, the CUSUM chart depicts the accumulation of information of several samples (current and previous samples). This feature of the CUSUM chart has made it a better chart than the X-bar chart for identifying small shifts in the process mean. However, the CUSUM chart is less powerful detecting rapid, large shifts.

The CUSUM chart is effective with samples of size n = 1, which makes it a better option for use in food processes in which rational subgroups are frequently of size 1, and in discrete part manufacturing with automatic measurement of each part and online process monitoring directly at the work centre. In this section, we concentrate on the CUSUM chart for the process mean. It is possible to plan CUSUM procedures for other type of variables, such as Poisson and binomial variables for modelling nonconformities and fraction nonconforming. A visual procedure proposed by Barnard in 1959, known as the V-Mask, is sometimes applied to determine whether a process is out-of-control. Commonly, the tabular form of the V-Mask is preferred. A V-Mask is an overlaid shape similar to a V shape on its side that is place over on the CUSUMs' graph. The original point of the V-Mask is placed on top of the latest CUSUM point, and past points are examined to see if any fall above or below the sides of the V. If the previous points fall between the sides of the V, the process is determined to be under statistical control or stable. Otherwise (if one point falls outside), the process is detected of being out-of-control.

Although CUSUM chart has a superior advantage against small shifts, the charts are not very popular as the chart is considerably more complicated to devise. Secondly, basic CUSUM chart does not detect large shifts quickly enough, and many users are more concerned about large shifts than about small ones. Finally, a critical issue with CUSUM charts is that most of the publication on the application of the chart, is based on inaccurate risk calculations (for more details see Woodall and Adams (1993)). As a result, the actual performance of many implementations of these charts is not similar as advertised, including the performance of several software packages.

5.8.8 Attribute Control Chart

Attribute control charts are the charts depicting the go or no-go or count information, which includes the number of defective units, the number of defects in a unit, the number of complaints received from dissatisfied customers, and the bacteria count found in the food sample. Attribute control charts are suitable when related to attribute data (male and female) and when theoretical distributions almost fit the model. Another type of attribute is conformance of the product/process with the target. The measurement of the data is typically based on continuous variables; for example, when the diameter of the sweets is over the limit, then the attribute is 'defective'. The control charts for individuals which were discussed in prior sections are based on a normal distribution; however, the attribute control chart is based on a different distribution.

Nevertheless, the patterns and rules to indicate an out-of-control condition are similar for both variables and attribute control charts. Similar to the variable control chart, the attribute control chart consists of several types of charts, depending on the types of data and the purpose of the process control.

A key disadvantage of an attribute control chart is that it loses the opportunity to acquire lots of information during the transformation of continuous measurements to attributes.

5.8.8.1 Proportion Defective Chart (p-Chart)

The proportion defective control chart (p-chart) is also known as a percent chart, a fraction nonconforming chart, a fraction defective chart, or simply as a p-chart. ASQ (American Society for Quality) defines a p-chart as a 'control chart for evaluating the stability of a process regarding the percentage (or proportion) of the total number of units in a sample in which an event of a given classification occurs'. The p-chart is used to detect and identify the percentage defective in each subgroup.

The items may have several quality characteristics that are examined simultaneously by the inspector. If the item does not conform to a standard on one or more of these characteristics, it is classified as nonconforming. How does it work? Instead of considering the number of defects that a unit might have, it identifies the unit as defective even if it has at least one defect. The measurement unit being examined is conforming (acceptable) or nonconforming (defective), where the binomial distribution is the basis for the chart.

The p-chart is often used when large quantities of products are manufactured relatively quickly. One advantage of the p-chart is that it can be used with both fixed and variable sample sizes. However, there are many instances in which sample sizes will vary, especially in the service sectors. If the sample consists of all the items produced during a period, it is likely that the sample size will vary and when that happens, the control limits are adjusted for each sample.

5.8.8.2 Number Defective Chart (np-Chart)

An alternative to the p-chart is the np-chart. The number defective control chart is also known as an np-chart. Compared to the p-chart, the np-chart is a control chart for assessing the stability of a process regarding the total number of units in a sample in which an event of a given classification occurs. It is sensitive to changes in the number of defective units in the measurement process. Similar to the p-chart, the 'event of a given classification' is whether the unit being examined is conforming (acceptable) or nonconforming (defective). The basis of the np-chart is considered binomial.

Criteria to use the np-chart are as follows:

- The *n* items counted are the number of items of those n items that fail to conform to the specification.
- Assume that *p* is the probability that an item will fail to conform to the specification; the value of p must be similar for each of the *n* items in a single sample.

Compared to the p-chart, the np-chart deals with the number, instead of the proportion, of defects/nonconforming products in each sample. Therefore, each sample size must remain constant. As with the p-chart, the np-chart is often used when large quantities of products are produced relatively quickly and provides the same advantages and disadvantages as the p-chart. The main advantage of the np-chart over the p-chart is the ease of understanding. Since the number of nonconforming units per sample is plotted on the chart, it provides direct evidence of the quantity of nonconforming products being produced in units. Operators commonly find the number of units easier to understand than proportions. A disadvantage of the np-chart compared to the p-chart is the inability of the chart to handle variable sample sizes. The patterns in both charts are identical, and both have equal power to respond to out-of-control conditions in the process.

5.8.8.3 c-Chart

The count chart or the number of nonconformities chart, which is also commonly known as the c-chart, is an attribute control chart applied to assess the stability of a process regarding the count of nonconformities occurring in a sample. It was applied to determine the variation in the number of defects in a constant sample size.

The main concern about the c-chart is the number of defects that are present in a sample, not with how many nonconforming units are present. Poisson distribution is the basis for the c-chart. In order to apply the c-chart, the occasions for defects to occur in the subgroup must be very large, but the number that occurs is small. For example, the opportunity for violation of food safety to occur in a plant is very large, but the number that occurs is small. One of the assumptions is that each inspection unit must always represent an identical area of opportunity for the occurrence of nonconformities. Also, nonconformities can be found in several different types on one unit, as long as the above conditions are satisfied for each category of nonconformity. In most practical situations, the violation of assumptions for the charts commonly happened. For example, the number of chances for the occurrence of nonconformities may be finite, or the probability of nonconformity occurrences may not be constant. As long as these departures from the assumptions are not severe, the Poisson model will usually work reasonably well.

5.8.8.4   U-Chart

The U-chart, which is also called the count chart per unit, is almost similar to the c-chart, which assesses the stability of a process in terms of the count of events of a given classification occurring per unit in a sample. Compared to the c-chart, which uses a constant sample size, the U-chart allows for the application of variable sizes of samples. Similar to the c-chart, the U-chart is applied when it is concerned with the number of nonconformities that are present in a sample, not with how many nonconforming units are present. Poisson distribution is the basis for the U-chart. It is common in practice that the sample size varies. For example, in manufacturing, when an inspection is done of an entire population, instead of samples taken from the population, the sample size frequently varies. However, what if the sample size in each subgroup is different? For such a case, information about defects needs to be plotted. Rather than a c-chart, a U-chart is more appropriate. A U-chart is applied as an alternative to the c-chart, as it only allows a constant subgroup size.

5.8.9   Run Chart

The run chart is a simple yet powerful tool in process improvement initiatives. It is a line graph of data plotted over time with median as a horizontal line. The run chart is useful at the beginning of a project as it depicts important information and process trends before there is sufficient data to calculate reliable control

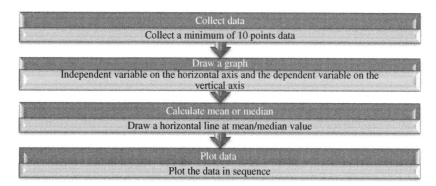

Figure 5.9 Steps in developing run chart.

limits. The key purpose to application of the run chart is to detect trends in processes weather there is an improvement or degradation of a process, which later may be detected by control charts for non-random pattern in the data. Figure 5.9 provide the steps to construct the chart.

5.8.10 Interpreting Control Chart Signals

In the following steps after the control chart development, the chart should be interpreted to understand the condition of the process regarding its stability and variability. The most common decision rule applied to classify whether the process is under control or not is by identifying if any points fall outside of the critical control limits. Common problems causing such out-of-control situations include changing to the poor quality of raw materials and an inexperienced operator replacing a well-trained operator.

Let us say that the process that we are monitoring shows no points outside the control limits. Are we 100% sure that the process is actually under control? The answer is no. The process may depict a non-random pattern, which indicates an out-of-control situation. Therefore, if managers decided to be stricter with the rules to identify a stable process, there are other decision rules that can be applied to control chart pattern assessment. We call it a non-random pattern, which can be used against the decision rules in Table 5.2.

5.8.11 Rules for Interpreting a Control Chart

The ability to interpret a particular pattern for assignable causes requires experience and sufficient knowledge of the process. Interpreting results is similar to the process talking to us about how the process is behaving. The information

Table 5.2 Rules for interpreting a control chart.

Western electric rules

- Any single data point falls outside the 3σ limit from the centreline
- Two out of three consecutive points plot beyond the 2σ limit (same side)
- Three consecutive points fall above the 1σ limit
- Seven consecutive points fall above the centreline
- Ten consecutive points fall below the centreline
- Six consecutive points fall below the 1σ limit
- Four consecutive points fall below the 2σ limit

AIAG rules

- One of one point is outside the ±3sigma control limits
- Seven out of seven points are above or below the centreline
- Seven points in a row are increasing
- Seven points in a row are decreasing

Juran rules

- One of one point is outside the ±3-sigma control limits
- Two of three points are above the 2-sigma control limits
- Two of three points are below the −2-sigma control limits
- Four of five points are above the 1-sigma control limits
- Four of five points are below the −1-sigma control limits
- Six points in a row are increasing
- Six points in a row are decreasing
- Nine out of nine points are above or below the centreline
- Eight points in a row are on both sides of the centreline, none in zone C

---

of the process depends upon the ability to read and deduce what the process is trying to convey.

The usual practice for control chart application in the industry is that of continual monitoring of key processes in the business. However, how about the companies that do not have the luxury of implementing a control chart at every key process? Realistically, not every process requires being monitored. If a process shows unwavering, stable control for a long time, it need not be monitored with the same zeal as one that frequently produces more defects and is more expensive. The SPC leader should avoid stable processes being charted, before the most critical process. In a mature quality management setting, less critical processes will have been monitored occasionally.

5.8.12 Where?

- Vendor control and selection
- Process and product specification conformance

- Sensory (colour, flavour, odour)
- Sort, wash, clarify, heat, filter, mill
- Package integrity, code, feel, appearance
- Defects and wastage calculation
- Productivity
- Process performance
- Microbiology
- Product specification conformance
- Process, product, process performance
- Process, product, control planning

5.9   Common Mistakes

Although a control chart is common in quality management practices, many errors may risk the effectiveness of the control chart. One of the most common errors is the incorrect selection of the control chart. For example, a sales department intends to plot the number of complaints received during each month. Since the number of complaints is the type of data that can be counted or discrete, an attribute control chart, c-chart, is the most appropriate chart to be applied. In practice, there are many instances in which a variable control chart (individual chart and moving-range chart) plots this type of information. Other common errors in applying control charts are as follows:

- Wrong formula used to calculate control limits. However, the paradigm shift towards the usage of software and technology has minimised such error.
- Missing, poor or erroneous measurements. Most of the employees were neither trained nor were told of the importance of having correct and quality data collection.
- Data on charts are not current. Common practice uses historical data for reporting and records. However, charts were not applied to prevent defective occurrences.
- Process adjustments have not been recorded.
- Special-cause signals were ignored, assuming that there is an error in the control chart.
- Non-random patterns were not studied, as it is common practice in the industry to assume that all their processes are under normal probability.
- Specification limits were placed on the chart instead of control limits. The consequences are that the control chart limits are widened and less stringent than it should. Subsequently, the control chart failed to raise the out-of-control warning.

5.10 Summary

- As SPC is known as a technique, there are some quality and statistical tools able to facilitate the SPC implementation.
- Not all the quality tools are required to be applied within the SPC implementation.
- A control chart is the core tool of SPC. There are two types of control chart based on the nature of the data, which are variable control chart and attribute control chart.

6

Team Formation, Team Dynamics and Training

6.1   The Team

SPC (Statistical Process Control) is a statistical and systematic technique for quality control and process improvement, requiring a group of people to deploy the technique in an organisation. One of the common challenges of implementation is that in this industry, only one person is responsible for it, which leads to the fact that SPC deployment works more efficiently with teamwork commitment. No matter how good engineers and statisticians or software programs are, it is impossible to improve quality without the participation of a functional company workforce – SPC relies heavily on the effectiveness and functional of a team.

Most of the food organisations have developed their teams to oversee quality-related issues even prior to the introduction of SPC deployment. For example, during the efforts of a company preparing itself for hazard analysis critical control point (HACCP) certification, according to the manual, a HACCP team must be developed to spearhead the certification process in a company. Commonly, the team has to change the operational and functional aspects following the SPC's mechanism and its underlying philosophy (Dogdu, Santos, and Dougherty 1997). The good news is that the mechanism of implementing SPC and HACCP has similarities, which means that team members can be allocated for both implementations.

The purpose of this study is to address the research gap in SPC implementation literature by answering the following research questions: 'What are the common team roles constituted in the SPC team?' and 'What are the characteristics of an SPC team that contribute to the team's effectiveness?'

Although teamwork is considered one of the critical success factors (CSFs) and team formation is numerously suggested in the roadmap of SPC implementation, there should be a recipe on the formation of the SPC team in a company. In order to reap the benefits of SPC, this chapter will highlight the importance of correct training at the right time; more importantly, incorporate the right people to form a multi-disciplinary team.

Statistical Process Control for the Food Industry: A Guide for Practitioners and Managers, First Edition.
Sarina Abdul Halim Lim and Jiju Antony.
© 2019 John Wiley & Sons Ltd. Published 2019 by John Wiley & Sons Ltd.

6.2 Team Dynamics

Team dynamics comprises of several components of a team:

- team structure,
- team roles/tasks, and
- team maturity

Recommended by practitioners and academicians as part of a continuous improvement effort, forming a well-established structure of a team will result in a successful team. Team roles/tasks are the generic activities that each team and its members execute for success.

6.2.1 Team Structure

Figure 6.1 depicted the types of teams encompasses the SPC team in an organisation, and later in Figure 6.2 depicts team members and their respective tasks (it is not compulsory to include all of the team members listed in the figure).

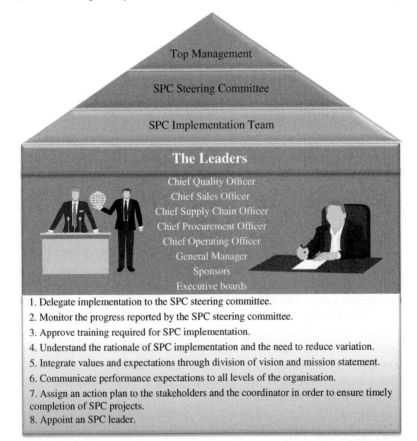

Figure 6.1 Types of SPC teams, team members and their tasks.

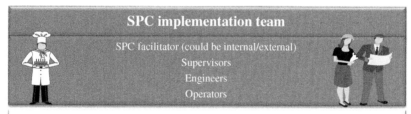

SPC Steering committee

SPC facilitator
Operation manager
Process manager
Quality manager
Quality improvement manager
Purchasing manager
Production manager
Maintenance manager
Reliability manager

1. Formulate goals and form teams.
2. Initiate training and programme support.
3. Set priorities for quality activities.
4. Stimulate SPC awareness through personal involvement.
5. Initiate promotion activities (e.g. SPC news and bulletin boards).
6. Stimulate team building.
7. Provide strategy for implementation.
8. Advise on quality strategy.
9. Assess results and certify teams when ready.
10. Make sure that the control plan is developed.
11. Provide an appropriate budget to realise improvement.
12. Monitor the progress of the SPC implementation team.
13. Assess problems and progress.
14. Report on progress to top management.
15. Apply cost–benefit analysis.

SPC implementation team

SPC facilitator (could be internal/external)
Supervisors
Engineers
Operators

1. Bring the process under control.
2. Implement the SPC project.
3. Resolve out-of-control situations.

Figure 6.1 (*Continued*)

SPC Coordinator

- A SPC coordinator is one of the critical roles — SPC deployment is prepared and planned not only to align the implementation with leaders' vision, but also to communicate the vision across the company
- **(Dogduetal., 1997; Hewson, Cox, and Stenning, 1997; Kumar and Gupta, 1993).**

Leader

- Someone who has a great interest in implementing SPC and is able to lead the team with a high level of commitment.
- A motivator that guides team members in problem solving by providing relevant materials and clear objectives of the SPC implementation.
- An important role in creating a creative-thinking culture when developing teams
- **(Gordon, Philpot, Bounds, and Long, 1994; Hewson, O'Sullivan, and Stenning, 1996; Krumwiede and Sheu, 1996; Watson, 1998).**

Sponsor

- SPC implementation requires investment from the organisation; thus, the availability of sponsors during the SPC project is vital to in ensuring smooth implementation.
- Sponsors may be required to provide a variety of resources including financial resources, allocating sufficient time for employees to run SPC projects, and the adequate workforce and technology required to carry out the project
- **(Bunney and Dale, 1997; Krumwiede and Sheu, 1996; Owen, Dale, and Shaw, 1989).**

SPC Expert

- This role may be selected internally or externally, depending on the organisation. However, as time goes by, the organisation should increase internal expertise based on organisational learning culture, instead of constantly depending on external expertise, which is costly for continuous implementation. A SPC expert plays a crucial role in providing knowledge and guidance related to SPC for the organisation to operate SPC as part ofits processes
- **(Antony and Taner, 2003; Does and Trip, 1997; Hewson et al., 1996).**

Users

- It is vital that this role be included in a SPC team, as they are the people who will continuously face and implement SPC in their processes. Furthermore, inputs from users are crucial because they are the right people to seek related process information, as they deal with processes all the time
- **(Does and Trip, 1997; Dogduetal., 1997; Kumar, 1993; Owen et al., 1989).**

Figure 6.2 SPC team members' roles.

Team members should be selected based on Figure 6.1, depending on the association of the team members with the process. The type of employee position is not the only factor necessary for implementation, but also individual roles (Meredith 1997; Senior 1997).

According to Belbin's roles theory, regardless of the size of the team, team roles should be assigned to team members (Figure 6.2). A good SPC team typically consists of a small team (six to eight) of people (Does, Roes, and Trip 1999). However, this has to correlate with the size of the company and the complexity of the project to facilitate the team in achieving agreed decisions efficiently.

A team operates most effectively, if the right combination of roles is present, which therefore the team roles and tasks were suggested in Figure 6.2.

6.2.2   SPC Team Characteristics

Teamwork involves interdependent tasks, and that team-level factors may be important in overall team performance. Related factors involved are:

- team performance
- strategies, coordination losses
- team cohesiveness
- group identity
- experience of working together

The most prominent characteristic found is multi-functional team (Antony 2000; Antony and Balbontin 2000; Antony and Taner 2003; Does and Trip 1997; Kumar and Motwani 1996; Kumar and Gupta 1993). These functions promote a cross-disciplinary flow of information in real-time problem solving (Mitra 2012). Functional diversity of a team should facilitate the team's ability to interact across team boundaries with members' home department, which leads to a positive effect on performance, as depicted in Table 6.1 (Cohen and Bailey 1997; Hackman 1987)

Involvement of a cross-functional team works very well in expanding SPC efforts in other departments, especially sharing of ideas and the obligation to participate (Kumar and Gupta 1993). Thus, each member feels a sense of achievement/satisfaction that his or her experience and opinions are adding value and contributing towards the organisational goal.

It is suggested that size has a curvilinear or inverted-U-shaped relation with team effectiveness; that too few or too many members impact a team's performance (Cohen and Bailey 1997). In the case of too few members, a printed circuit board case study wherein a team of two to three people are described as having an insufficient number to induce better ideas from each other Dogdu,

Table 6.1 Team effectiveness criteria.

Team effectiveness	Description
Output	• The outcome of the workgroup should meet or exceed the performance standards of the people who receive and review the output. • The effectiveness of a team implies that the team's output should be able to be accepted by the managers or clients who are evaluating its performance.
Social process	• The processes involved in carrying out the work should maintain or enhance the capability of members to work together on completing team tasks. • Some groups operate in such a way that the group integrity as a performing unit is destroyed in the process of performing the task, which indicates the ineffectiveness of a team.
The group experience	• The group is on balance, satisfy rather than frustrate the personal needs of group members. • If the effect of team membership is to keep individuals from doing what they desire or need to do, then the cost of generating the team products is probably too high.
Performance	• Efficiency, productivity, response times, quality, customer satisfaction
Attitude	• Employee satisfaction, commitment, and trust in management
Behavioural outcomes	• Absenteeism, turnover and safety

Santos, and Dougherty (1997). Dale and Shaw (1992) suggested that a small team of people comprising production, technology, quality and maintenance oversee the implementation developed. On the contrary, Harris (1994) argues that successful SPC implementation projects consist of a larger team size, compared to unsuccessful SPC implementation projects which consist of a smaller size. Based on a study involving 72 employees by Magjuka and Baldwin (1991), increasing the team size (8–46 members) was suggested, which implies fewer sub-units of the team; thus, fewer leaders are required to manage the team. However, it is also arguable that the bigger the size of the team, the more complex the factors that need to be handled, affecting team effectiveness in SPC implementation (Hackman 1987).

Within the SPC implementation project, the success of the implementation is highly dependent on the task assignments. It is imperative to decide how the division of tasks among team members impact both the efficiency of task performance and the efficiency of knowledge acquisition (Elg, Olsson, and Dahlgaard 2008; Hutchins 1997). Despite the fact that teamwork is a practice in the industry (Antony and Balbontin 2000), having the skills to deal with team interaction and to function within specific team roles requires careful attention as well.

Members of SPC team are often suggested to be permanent members in the implementation process, and preferably without having a change in group members. However, for the SMEs (Small, medium enterprise) flexibility of changing team members is essential. Moreover, the same people working together on long-term projects eventually lose their interest and efficiency after some time. Furthermore, some of the characteristics which have not been explicitly discussed in SPC, but instead in quality management in general, are considered as well. One is the selection of the right people in the team. Common factors for a successful team are management support, training quality, team techniques, a stated mission, interdepartmental membership, financial resources, and empowerment.

6.2.3   Team Maturity

Most teams are said to follow a path on their way towards excellent performance; teams start with a collection of strangers and become united with common goals. In 1965, psychologist Bruce Tuckman first came up with the distinct stages of 'forming, storming, norming, and performing' to reflect the stages of team maturity (Tuckman and Jensen 1977). Bruce Tuckman and Mary Ann Jensen have added the adjourning or mourning phase, reflecting a wrapping-up task which breaks up the team. However, as SPC is a continuous activity, this stage of the team is not favourable. According to Elrod and Tippett (1999), listed several characteristics on team maturity, which are:

* Respects to all team members
* Effective individual and team communications
* Coordinated development and alignment of individual and team goals
* Recognition and reward of teamwork

Figure 6.3 display the team maturity stages for the team involved in SPC projects.

The stages involves the forming level of the team, the development of a stable team and finally at the real team stage, the team is able to work as a cohesive unit. However, if the team members has gone through changes, the team maturity is back to the first stage. They were developed for cross-functional teams for specific purposes (for implementing SPC within the company in this case), and applicable for audit teams. The Figure 6.4 will the role of a leader in transforming a team in SPC projects.

This chapter also provides tips on how to move from each stage as depicted in Figure 6.5. As SPC leader is also recognised as the CSF for SPC implementation, the role of a leader in spearheading the team towards a mature team. Managers

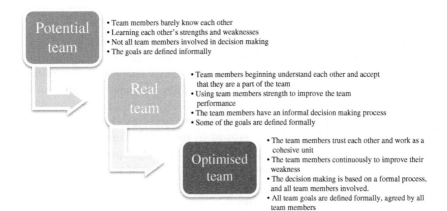

Figure 6.3 SPC Team maturity.

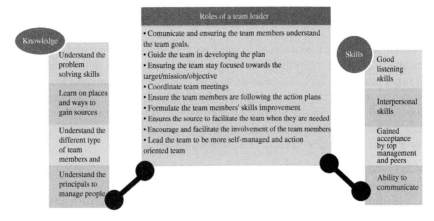

Figure 6.4 The roles of a leader in a team.

are able to identify the maturity of their current team, and the behaviours and tasks of the leader along the SPC project as depicted in the Figure 6.4.

6.3 Training

Training is always required, whether to initiate a new quality management system or to sustain current performance. Food safety training is the most common and basic training provided, which meant that training in quality techniques are assumed less important. Compared to the SPC companies, non-SPC companies offered less training opportunities for quality improvement techniques. These companies mostly define food quality as food safety

• Did the participants
apply the knowledge
and skills?

• Did the
participants
understand the
concept or the
skills?

• Any improvement
on the processes
and organisational
performance?

• Did the
participants
able to teach
the knowledge
or skills they
acquired?

• Did the training
cost balance with
the output of the
training?

• Did the participants
apply the knowledge
and skills?

Figure 6.5 Training evaluation criteria.

due to their obligation to comply with food laws and regulations. Therefore, training in quality improvement is considered less important than food safety training (Dora et al. 2013a,b; Lim, Antony, and Albliwi 2014).

In order to ensure the success of SPC implementation, knowing food safety is insufficient for implementation purposes. It is essential that everyone in the company not only be aware of SPC but also to understand the importance of SPC, and how it can be advantageous to employees and the company?. Top management awareness of SPC is crucial and should be introduced with an emphasis on definitions, requirements and benefits. In the food industry, training for quality management was high concerning to the food safety, and therefore in SPC training is often a part of the FQM (Food quality management) training modules.

The objectives of training programmes in SPC implementation are to:

• Understand the variation and types of variation (assignable cause or common cause)
• Understand the steps in identifying the root cause of the assignable cause variation
• Increase awareness of quality and SPC tools

- Reduce the resistance to SPC adoption
- Maintain in-house expertise in relation to SPC implementation
- Support the sustainability of SPC implementation and establish a continuous learning culture in the company

Most training sessions mainly focus on the technical aspects, neglecting the managerial aspects, which often cause the failure of SPC implementation (Hoerl 1995). The technical aspect are referring to the statistical component SPC (e.g. formulation, sampling, assumptions). The most ineffective approach is to provide all information in one training session. On the other hand, to provide training at each step of the implementation will cost the company more time and money.

Ensuring that the module of training matches the level of employees' knowledge is essential, as the food industry workforce was found to be lacking in knowledge and statistical skills. The trainer is highly advised to make sure that the survey of employees in a company reveals their special skills, knowledge, interests and motivations, which could be used to enrich and maximise the role of employees in SPC. In order to increase its effectiveness and efficiently use the resources (time, cost), the level of SPC training, as depicted in Table 6.2, is divided into three levels and each will be trained with the respective level of training materials.

For smaller food companies, a collaborative effort is suggested especially collaborating with other organisations/businesses, customers or government bodies/academic institutions. In a typical food manufacturing company, the majority of training and learning takes place on the site, not in the classroom. Therefore, a continuous improvement manager is necessary to

Table 6.2 SPC training programme.

Characteristics	Level 1	Level 2	Level 3
Objective	• Provide general concepts of SPC without technical details	• Develop problem-solving skills and teamwork	• Guide the application of a control chart and (out-of-control action plan) OCAP
Participants	• All employees	• SPC steering team	• SPC steering team, SPC implementation team and related personnel to the selected process
Contents	• Statistical thinking • Quality tools • Overview of process performance • Measurement system	• Data quality and SPC tools and the relation of these tools to current QC/manufacturing practices	• Theoretical and hands-on approach to control charts • Sampling and data collection methods • Capability analysis, OCAP and emphasis on data analysis and feedback action

encourage supervisors and management to include quality concepts in their training efforts.

6.4 Consultant

Training must be customised according to the company and planning it, is one of the more time-consuming elements of the implementation. For a new SPC user, management will typically depend on an external consultancy company, as most of them have developed a comprehensive SPC training programme. At this point, managers should select the consulting company, as there are various types of training modules which the consulting company will offer that is appropriate with the employees' level of knowledge. The consulting company may design the training plan for them to run the training at the food company. The usage of the consultant can be replaced by an in-house trainer with increasing maturity in using SPC in the business. Food companies are also suggested to seek external advice from academic institutes. Local universities can facilitate food companies in several ways in embarking on their CI (Continuous improvement) journey, such as training (e.g. statistics and its applications), principles of SPC, tools and techniques of CI. Student internship works on SPC or Six Sigma projects supported by an academic mentor, and work with the knowledge transfer programme. In the UK, Knowledge Transfer Partnerships (KPTs) is implemented in the UK-wide with objective to help businesses to improve their productivity, competitiveness and growth. This government-funded programme is implemented to encourage collaborations between businesses and the universities in the UK. Each of the KPT will involve three partners which are the business/company, education institution or research organisation and an associate.

6.5 Follow-Up in-House Training

Preferably, an in-house expert will lead the training by designing and planning the implementation programme. A strategic approach is to start small and build up a bank of knowledge and experience. The SPC tools should be introduced together with the existing methods of process control, which exist in the company. Similar to a quasi-experimental approach, this allows the team to make comparisons of the process performance between the new and old methods. Such comparisons will be effectively building the confidence of employees towards the advantages of implementing SPC. The success of improving a few operations using SPC will rapidly establish the technique as a trusted and capable method for understanding, monitoring, controlling and improving the processes in the business.

With an effective training programme, follow-ups are viewed as vital not only in validating the effectiveness of previous training sessions but also in updating new information related to SPC and process management. Follow-up training is typically followed up within six to eight weeks for a workshop of one to two days. The follow-up training sessions are also effective in providing feedback on previous project efforts. The wider presence of top management and senior management will further encourage the follow-up activities.

Key question: 'How do we evaluate training effectiveness?'

6.6 Measuring Training Effectiveness

Each training session invests money, people and time; therefore, any organisation should and must evaluate the effectiveness of the sessions. Every training programme offered by the organisation must achieve positive results or it should be modified until acceptable results are achieved. A training session should enhance the method or process of executing a particular task of the process; if not, the training is not effective. The assessment should be done upon completion of the training and not necessarily as an end-course survey. One of the effective approaches is using a cost–benefit ratio. Training is an activity of transferring knowledge from a learning environment to real practice. Therefore, the evaluation criteria should be precisely focused on measuring the effectiveness of the knowledge transfer.

- A realistic duration for training is one to two days with several follow-up sessions, as the audience will start to lose concentration if it is longer than that.
- Several days' break between each session of the training, with a hands-on experience being given.
- Do not overwhelm the employees, as this statistical business is new to most of them.

Successful training indicates the participants effectively apply the knowledge and display good motivation and skills gained in the training session (Kontoghiorghes 2001). One of the approaches to evaluating the effectiveness of training is the Kirkpatrick model. Kirkpatrick Evaluation Model developed by Donald Kirkpatrick, and it has been used as a fundamental model for the detection and targeting of training-specific interventions in organisations. Kirkpatrick (1979) stressed that an appraisal of training should go beyond direct reactions of attendees.

Level 1: Reaction

- Level 1 solicits thoughts and suggestions of the learning experience following a training event or course. The feedback from the participants identifies the degree to which the experience was valuable, relevant and satisfying.
- Feedback is valuable for the trainers in evaluating the effectiveness of training sessions and materials, participants' opinions, and in continuously seizing opportunities for improvement.
- Such evaluations, however, does not measure what participants have learned but instead focuses on the interest, motivation and attention level of participants.

Level 2: Learning

- Level 2 measures the degree to which the training achieves the target of the session.
- Only by determining what trainees are learning, and what they are not, can organisations make necessary improvements.
- The cognitive improvement of trainees was assessed at this point.
- Learning assessments can be in written assessments or role-plays to demonstrate the participants' skills.
- The assessment can take place as pre-training and post-training assessment of the knowledge gained from the training sessions.

Level 3: Behaviour

- Level 3 assesses the behavioural/attitudinal change of the participants due to the training – basically whether the knowledge and skills from the training are then applied in their daily work environment.
- This involves assessment of the ability of the trainees to use their newly learned knowledge or skills in the workplace.
- The assessment at this level depicts the reflection of how much the participant was influenced by the training material. Please note that it is not necessarily a direct assessment tool.
- A change in behaviour can be due to a variety of other reasons, such as an individual's reluctance to change.
- Similarly, this level of assessment involves both pre- and post-training measurement of the participant's behaviour.

Level 4: Results

- This is the level where management measures the overall training impact, including financial or moral impact.
- Training results (measurable and tangible) include quality improvement, variation reduction, cost reduction, increased productivity, employee turnover, employee retention, increased sales, and elevated motivation.

- The assessment enables managers to identify the critical return on investment of their training expenses.
- The most common difficulty is in identifying whether the outcomes are the actual results of the training.
- This level involves assessing both pre- and post-event measurement of the training objectives.

After a training session has ended, the SPC leader may assess the effectiveness of the training session using the criteria depicted in Figure 6.5, which adapted from the Kirkpatrick Evaluation Model. However, it is clear that the in SPC implementation, one of the training session is to develop in-house expertise in SPC. Therefore, the ability of the participants to teach others is critical not only to expand the numbers of skilled employees, but also this shows the participants understand and able to apply the knowledge and skill themselves. Another category, which is return on investment is clearly important for the business to implement only effective trainings as a strategic approach for business excellence.

Training in SPC is viewed to be more effective when implemented in a participative company in which management not only encourage the employees to learn and apply the skills and knowledge they learned in training sessions but also recognise or rewarding their efforts. Therefore, successful training is dependent on the training design, facilitators, management support, and the prevailing knowledge transfer climate.

6.7 Summary

- It is impossible to have a successful SPC programme without having good teamwork commitment, as SPC highly relies on the input and participation of a functional company workforce.
- The structure of the SPC team may include three sub-teams: top-management team, steering team and SPC implementation team – each respective team has different tasks within the SPC implementation.
- Each SPC team member should be assigned roles that are important to ensure that the team is functional in the implementation of SPC, which comprises the leader, sponsors, SPC expert, SPC coordinator, and users.
- It is important that team performance to be assessed and improved. Several factors known to contribute towards team performance are deep strategies, coordination losses, cohesiveness, group identity, and experience of working together.
- The maturity of a team is viewed to be transformative (e.g. forming, storming, norming and performing) in the long term.

- As training sessions are vital to SPC implementation, structured and properly planned training is highly suggested. Commonly, SPC training will be implemented in different stages according to different levels of position in the company.
- The training sessions' effectiveness must be assessed. One of the approaches is the Kirkpatrick Evaluation Model, which comprises four criteria: reaction, learning, behaviour and results.

7

SPC Readiness Self-Assessment Tool

7.1 Ready....?

A failure to establish sufficient readiness represented half of all unsuccessful efforts towards organisational change
(Gurumurthy, Mazumdar, Muthusubramanian 2013)

Initiating the Statistical Process Control (SPC) programme in business indicates that there is a demand for change from the common practice. Thus, managing change is very important at each level. Moreover, it is more critical for the management to assess the organisational readiness before planning to manage the change. Nevertheless, The SPC implementation in the food industry is slow despite the success of SPC in the manufacturing industry (e.g. the automotive industry) (Grigg and Walls 2007a,b; Lim, Antony, & Albliwi, 2014).

Similar to other CI tools/techniques, organisational readiness is an essential ingredient required for effective and sustainable use of SPC (Radnor 2011). In general, the company-wide SPC application is challenged by the resistance of employees to organisational changes (Surak 1999). Therefore, it is crucial to consider organisation preparedness to undertake SPC, and this can be determined by assessing its readiness level (Antony 2014; Lagrosen, Chebl, and Tuesta, 2011; Smith 2005). The readiness assessment is an approach for overcoming any resistance to change (a critical factor challenging the adoption of the technique) (Holt et al. 2007; Kerlinger 1986; Smith 2005; Xie and Goh 1999). The readiness phase is similar to the 'unfreezing' phase conceptualised by Lewin (1947), in which members of the organisation are encouraged to relinquish, both physically and psychologically, existing practices for process control and improvement.

Failure to assess employees readiness often cause the managers to spend a considerable amount of time dealing with resistance towards change (Abdolvand, Albadvi, and Ferdowsi, 2008; Antony 2014; Coch and French Jr. 1948; Lee and Lee 2014; Self and Schraeder 2009). By ensuring organisational

Statistical Process Control for the Food Industry: A Guide for Practitioners and Managers, First Edition.
Sarina Abdul Halim Lim and Jiju Antony.

readiness before attempting to adopt SPC, the organisation does not need coping mechanisms to deal with employees' resistance during and after the implementation of such a process (Coch and French Jr. 1948; Kotter 2008a,b; Kotter and Schlesinger 2008; Self and Schraeder 2009). Thus, creating readiness for SPC adoption also encourages positive force and, consecutively, significantly improves the adoption behaviours.

Get-set... go!

Regardless of the direction of changes, it is imperative to assess:

- The readiness of the people;
- The willingness to embrace change; and
- The capability to implement change.
- How ready people are for the change?
- How willingly people to embrace the change?
- How capable people to implement the change?

7.2   Concept of Readiness

The readiness concept has been an understudied topic until now; there is no general definition of readiness given. Nevertheless, in organisational studies, readiness is an important study under organisational change theories where several researchers provide different definitions of readiness (see Figure 7.1).

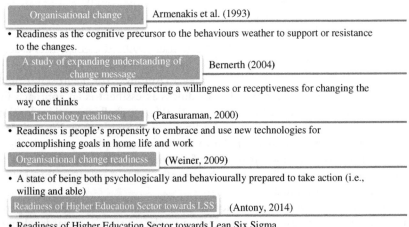

Figure 7.1 Concept of readiness.

SPC readiness is defined as the organisational ability to accept and support the initiation of SPC as common practice for successfully implement SPC and to sustaining stability of their processes.

7.3 History of the Readiness Concept

Originally, the idea of preparedness was directly linked to the context of managers' actions towards addressing the issue of employees' resistance to change. The primary findings by Coch and French (1948) suggested the idea that managers could reduce their employees' resistance to change. Moreover, the term 'readiness' was pioneered by Jacobson (1957), which was presented in a study emphasising on resistance to change. Furthermore, he stated that *'there is no analysis of readiness and no extended discussion on successful change'* despite the resistance to change had frequently been discussed. Thus, it was suggested that 'openness to change' is a similar concept to 'readiness', which should be viewed as one's internal attitude that precedes behaviour when supporting or resisting change. On the other hand, 'resistance' refers to external behaviours or actions taken to stop, delay, or otherwise jeopardise the successful implementation of an organisational change. Therefore, Holt et al. (2007) reinforced the idea that readiness is a different approach to deal with resistance, and should be conceptualised as the antecedent to behaviours related to adoption or resistance of change.

Similar to SPC implementation, which was considered a new technology to be adopted in the food company, resistance to change was discovered to be the biggest barrier towards a successful SPC implementation in the industry (Lim, Antony, & Albliwi, 2014; Surak 1999). Therefore, based on the organisational theories explained above, the 'readiness' phase is significant to reduce the resistance to change (see Figure 7.2). Hence, a three-stage model of change depicted that change must be initiated at the 'unfreezing phase', whereby the organisation transforms the existing mindset and develops the motivation to change. Actions thought to create readiness for change (i.e. unfreezing) include brief a clear information to the organisation members of the current situation. Apart from that, such actions thought also motivate their discontent with the status quo, create an appealing vision of a future state of affairs, and foster a sense of confidence that this future state can be realised (Armenakis, Harris, & Mossholder, 1993).

Rusly, Corner, and Sun (2012) explained that readiness for changes has three phases: (i) preparation for change, (ii) adoption of change, and (iii) institutionalisation of change. They also highlighted the fact that 'readiness' consists of both a state and a process, which was originally suggested in a study by Dalton and Gottlieb (2003). Thus, the integration of innovation diffusion and organisational change demonstrate readiness for change, as it is argued that both

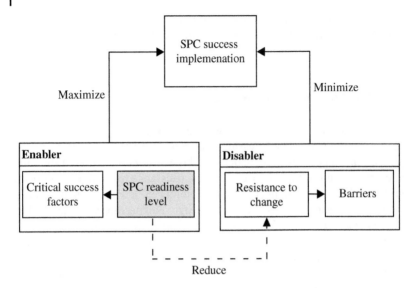

Figure 7.2 Positioning SPC readiness in SPC implementation.

Figure 7.3 The innovation diffusion for change process.

theories illustrate the importance of individual beliefs in successful organisational change (Rusly et al. 2012) (depicted in Figure 7.3).

However, how does innovation diffusion relating to adopting SPC in a company?

Based on 'readiness' studies through innovation diffusion (Rogers (1995), the organisational innovation combines the development and implementation of new ideas, systems, products, and technology.

- Clarke (1999): the diffusion process is the spread of a new idea from its source of invention or creation to its ultimate users or adopters.
- Harcourt and Brace (2011): refers to innovation as the act of introducing something new, in which a similar situation is depicted with SPC adoption, where food companies will be replacing the traditional way of managing process stability.
- (Ehigie and McAndrew 2005): in the innovation change process, the adoption is led by the first introduction or implementation of an innovation, which results from a diffusion process.

Therefore, in its core principle, SPC involves changes to organisational methods and practices to achieve the target of process performance. Similarly, Ahire and Ravichandran (2001) proposed an innovation diffusion framework of Total Quality Management (TQM) adoption, representing TQM as a management innovation.

7.4 An Approach to Assessing SPC Readiness in the Organisations

The topic relating to organisational readiness is under-researched in the CI (Continuous Improvement) literature. Organisational change theory posits that greater readiness increases the opportunity that new techniques will be implemented successfully (Antony 2014; Armenakis et al. 1993). Social cognitive theory suggests that when organisational readiness for change is high, the employees are more likely to initiate change (e.g. institute new practices such as SPC). Herscovitch and Meyer (2002) cited motivation theory to argue that when organisational readiness is high, employees will act to support changes in ways that exceed their job requirements or expected role. Moreover, Kotter (2008a,b) suggested that failure to establish sufficient organisational readiness wastes half of all efforts towards organisational change. Thus, it showed that the employees will exert greater effort in support of the change, and exhibit higher persistence in the face of obstacles or setbacks during implementation process (Bandura (1993); Weiner (2009).

The application of force field analysis (diagnostic process) is an approach that is relatively quick and effective to determine the preparedness of the business to apply SPC. As developed by Kurt Lewin, it is useful to focus on the variables involved in planning and implementing a change programme.

Force Field Analysis

1. Provide cards/post-it notes to the participants (executives/senior managers)
2. The participants will each list the factors that support and hinder the SPC implementation.
3. Each card will represent an issue.
4. Together with the facilitator, the factors should be grouped, and several themes will emerge.
5. Identify the strongest themes in supporting the implementation, critical obstacles hindering it.

(Continued)

(Continued)

Drivers	Restraints
Need to reduce waste	Resistance to change
Need to lower cost	Focused on short-term saving
Process oriented	Implement quick fix
Motivated employees	Lack of support of all levels
Need process improvement	Wrong perceptions of real problems
Require a systematic process control approach	Lack of knowledge on quality tools

It allows the determination of the strongest points to promote the SPC benefits in the company. Together with the benefits, force field analysis facilitates the company to identify the major obstacles and challenges that require attention to be addressed for a successful implementation.

7.5   Key Components of SPC Readiness

Another approach is to assess the SPC readiness through the key criteria as shown in the figure below. A tool known as SPC Readiness Assessment Tool was developed in a previous study for the purpose of focusing on measuring the preparedness of food companies while implementing SPC (Figure 7.4).

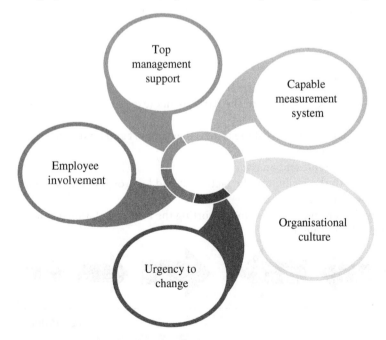

Figure 7.4 Components of SPC Readiness.

7.6 Top Management Support

Top management readiness is demonstrated by providing significant support towards SPC implementation. The top management should be convinced that SPC is a valuable instrument for improving process stability and capability for the top management to depict continual active and enthusiastic behaviour for the implementation. Two significant forms of support may occur in ensuring the company is ready for a successful SPC adoption, which provides a supportive climate and allocates necessary resources and investments for SPC. Nevertheless, the most common pitfall for the implementation is the top management has underestimated the commitment SPC requires or the top management fail to understand their roles in adopting SPC.

7.6.1 Capable Measurement System

The purpose of measurement system analysis is to verify whether the quality parameters are measured accurately to detect changes when the SPC team applies corrective action in improving the process. In general, the measurement system in the industry has not been assessed, and most of the managers underestimate the variations caused by the measurement system. Poor measurement system caused poor data quality. Thus, in the production line, the measurement system directly involves several significant components that require attention i.e. the employees, machinery and measuring tools. The mechanism of SPC is reflected through the critical use of data from the processes, highlighting the importance of having the most minimal error and variations in the measurement system

7.6.2 Organisational Culture

> We believe that most if not all of …failures of other such change initiatives-are not failures of management. Rather, they may have attributed to the fundamental, pervasive organisational CULTURE…
>
> (McNabb and Sepic 1995)

Culture dictates the type of behaviour. It also establishes the methods the problems are addressed, outlines how relationships are defined and supported, and establishes how work is conducted (Schein 2010). Therefore, culture is a crucial factor in all actions, operations, and relationships in the company. Organisational culture is imperative as the causal factor for the preparedness of a company towards the adoption of SPC. The culture of each organisation's quality management approach is unique and individual, depending on the maturity of the organisations. The culture of organisations determines the readiness for the acceptance of the philosophy underlying SPC. As such, the managers should comprehensively examine their organisational culture to increase the success while attempting to introduce any change in an organisation. The change involves alteration of employee's decision-making practices, interactions, and level of involvement in quality management and performance assessment. If the organisational culture tends to reject changes, any new initiatives will fail regardless of the top management intention and plans.

7.6.3 Employee Involvement

The application of SPC inevitably utilises total employee involvement in the day-to-day efforts for quality control activities. Thus, the employees who are exposed to quality improvement activities have a better understanding of the need to change their current practices to improve the acceptance of new changes. For instance, it was discovered that weekly team meetings permitted the employees to be trustworthy and open to changes. These meeting sessions enable them to discuss the changes and their subsequent implications with the manager. The employees with a higher level of participation and greater communication skills responded more positively to change.

The current practice commonly reflects how the supervisors who get used to the existing hierarchy and thus disapprove of the empowerment provided to the employees, in the form of actions and independent decision-making by the employees. Kotter and Schlesinger (2008) highlighted the crucial role of training in empowering the employees and Kotter (1996) had broad empirical support for this proclamation.

- A great example was reflected by Ford and its workers' union (United Auto Workers), whereby they created an effective training programme that emphasised the change of corporate culture in Ford. Training is a practical approach to develop a sense of responsibility and empowerment among the employees.
- An empirical case study on organisational change at Honeywell Inc. identified that forming team ownership and an employee involvement base is essential to assist in improving the change acceptance within the organisations (Paper, Rodger, and Pendharkar 2001).

Kerber and Buono (2005) suggested that *'the changes by adopting continuous improvement methods and breakthrough changes, is possible for motivating employees to initiate and experiment with changing. Such an approach encourages employees to lead, and this is essential for the change effort'* (Kotter 1996). As such, there can be profound outcomes reflected from their attitudes as this can provide them with some sense of responsibility for the change process and assist in moving the change effort along at least listening to the employees and allowing the employees to make decisions (Kappelman et al. 1993).

7.6.4 Urgency to Change

One factor emerged as pivotal: a sense of urgency. Thus, top management needs to be clear on the reason to invest in SPC implementation, which brought to the main question: *'Why do we need SPC?'* The food businesses usually apply SPC due to reaction purposes, which mostly due to the requirement by the customers or retailers. Typically, the companies that highlight the urgency for SPC uptake would indicate that the top management is highly motivated to improve the status quo – to seize opportunities, avoid hazards and eliminate low-priority activities to operate smoothly (Kotter 2008a,b).

As this is one of the most challenging steps in Kotter's eight-stage model of change, it is crucial in empowering managers to explain the need for change and tackle employee complacency (Kotter 2008a,b). A company must begin by evaluating its competitiveness, market position, financial performance and current technological trends before deciding whether to adopt SPC (Appelbaum et al. 2012). The food industry is highly resistant to SPC implementation due to fear and their unfamiliarity with statistical techniques. Compared to the employees in other sectors, they are rarely required to apply statistical techniques in their daily job (Dora et al. 2013a,b). Consequently, fire-fighting remains the prominent problem-solving approach in this sector (Hersleth and Bjerke 2001). Complacency is another significant issue in the food industry, which many companies underestimate its consequences and prevalence. It is critical to combat complacency and differentiates between true and false urgency, which often confusing. True urgency arises if the managers are highly motivated and passionate to seek relentlessly for opportunities to improve their status. Therefore, food companies must develop a sense of true urgency before they can adopt SPC. On the other hand, false urgency, which is usually the result of pressure from top management or customers, often leads to action, which does not address the root cause of the issues.

Common pitfalls

- Top management often underestimate the commitment required for implementing SPC;
- Unclear vision for the implementation process;
- Expect quick results;
- Vision of the implementation is not communicated well to the employees; and
- Provides little attention to the measurement system
- Too comfortable with current process performance

7.7 Identifying the Readiness Level

In general, the top management decides on the readiness of a company to implement SPC, where the judgements are mostly made based on their personal experience. Table 7.1 showed the usage of standard SPC assessment criteria to facilitate the company in making an objective decision on a holistic view of the organisation readiness level.

7.7.1 How to Use the SPC Readiness Assessment Tool?

The company's readiness score was compared to the Readiness Score Threshold as shown in Table 7.2, which depicted in the empirical study on SPC readiness as mentioned by Lim and Antony (2016). Thresholds to determine the level of readiness was equivalent to the characteristics of Kaye and Dyason's (1995) quality control model (era 2), Dale and Smith's (1997) quality management implementation grid (level 5-Improver) and Dale and Lascelles (1997) level 3-Tool pushers. Besides, Table 7.2 depicted that a score of 3 or above suggests that the organisation is ready to embrace SPC. A score below 2 indicated the need for remedial action. The average score of each readiness factor was determined to get the grand average readiness score for the company.

Development of the SPC Readiness Self-assessment Tool
The criteria in the SPC Readiness Self-assessment Tool is derived from a Delphi study. The study identified SPC readiness factors through two rounds of interviewing the SPC experts, where consensus opinion was identified. The study has validated the tool with multiple-case studies in the confectionery industry. The details of the study can be referred in (Lim and Antony 2016).

- Table 7.2 depicted that a score of 3 or above shows the organisation is ready to embrace SPC and should proceed to do so.
- The score in the Amber category, a score of 2 to 3 indicates that the company is not preparing to adopt SPC. Nevertheless, the company is expected to be sufficiently prepared after remedial action is taken to rectify factors with lower scores to improve the company readiness level. Typically, the corrective action required in this category is minimal.

Example 7.1 The final category is an alarming category as the company is significantly unprepared to initiate the investment in SPC adoption. Typically, the company needs major corrective action where the intention to adopt SPC should be put to a halt at this point in the final category.

Table 7.1 SPC readiness self-assessment tool.

SPC Readiness Self-Assessment Tool

---

0 = never implemented,
1 = rarely implemented,
2 = occasionally implemented,
3 = often implemented and
4 = always implemented.

Top management support	**Average Score**
T1	The management is ready to commit to SPC implementation (e.g. shut down a highly unstable process for corrective action, and provide resources to investigate and overcome the cause of the problem)	
T2	Top management understands its role and commits to start implementing SPC	
T3	Top management demands regular (e.g. daily, monthly) process performance reviews and holds monthly review sessions focusing on quality	
T4	Top management support CI activities	
T5	Top management visibly committed to SPC implementation	

Capable measurement system	**Average Score**
M1	The measurement system is available	
M2	Employees aware of the critical processes	
M3	Employees trained to collect data	
M4	Appropriate measurement tools exist	
M5	Guidelines are available for calibrating measuring equipment	

Organisational culture	**Average Score**
O1	Decision making is based on data	
O2	Problems are addressed using a teamwork approach	
O3	Process performance is measured using appropriate metrics (e.g. Cpk, Ppk)	
O4	Regular meetings (e.g. monthly) are held to discuss quality problems using data	
O5	Employees' accountability is respected, and blame culture discouraged	

Urgency to change	**Average Score**
U1	Top management communicates legitimate reasons for adopting SPC	
U2	Confidence that the company will benefit from SPC implementation; it will not just be introduced in response to customer demand	
U3	Understand that SPC able to continually improve process performance	

Employee involvement	**Average Score**
E1	Employees trained in basic statistics	
E2	Employees' ideas and opinions are appreciated	
E3	SPC facilitator hired (external/internal) to aid SPC adoption	
E4	Employees understand the benefits of process improvement to the business and themselves	
E5	Employees involved in CI activities	

Table 7.2 The SPC readiness score threshold.

Level of readiness	Mean	Description
	>3	Ready
		In the right state to initiate implementation
	2–3	Moderately ready
		The company should continue with its plan to adopt SPC but needs to reassess the readiness factors that gave a low score
	<2	Not ready
		Most of the factors score very low, indicating that the company may not be entirely prepared to commit to the adoption and implementation of SPC

Bakers, Ready for SPC?

A company produced baked snacks under several major brands in the UK and it produced digestive products, sweet biscuits and savoury snacks within the UK. The company had tried to implement Lean. Nevertheless, the initial implementation of Lean had little success as the implementation process failed to progress. The employees of the company did not accept the change that was introduced. One of the major issues with the production process is that there was high variability in the production, creating unstandardized products. The processes capability index was not assessed and the stability of the process is still unknown. The top management decided to adopt SPC to improve the process and to reduce the gap in high variability of products through the Continuous Quality Manager. Therefore, the company decided to assess their readiness to implement SPC. The Continuous Quality Manager completed the SPC Readiness Assessment Tool form. The results are shown in the spider graph below.

SPC Readiness Factors	Attributes					Average score
Top management support	T1	T2	T3	T4	T5	2.6
Score	3	2	3	2	2	
Capable measurement system	M1	M2	M3	M4	M5	2.6
Score	2	3	1	3	4	
Organisational culture readiness	O1	O2	O3	O4	O5	2
Score	2	2	1	3	2	
Sense of urgency	U1	U2	U3			3.3
Score	3	3	4			
Employee involvement	E1	E2	E3	E4	E4	1.6
Score	2	1	1	2	2	
GRAND AVERAGE SCORE						**2.73**

1. The result shows the Readiness score of each attribute.
2. The organisation has a high sense of urgency to implement SPC due to the high variation in the processes, which impacts the production efforts of the business.
3. The organisation minimised involvement of employee, especially when it came to improving the overall quality of goods produced. Most of the employees are foreign workers who often face difficulties in understanding and when communicating with managers. The employees are hesitant to convey and communicate their ideas as there is no effective medium for it. The employees perceive that the top management are not interested in hearing their suggestions.
4. The organisation has yet to establish the stability and capability of the process, therefore leaving a gap in the process capability value. The process capability value however, is not one of the process performance's measurement criteria.
5. The readiness level indicates that the company is moderately ready for the SPC implementation with an average score of 2.73 (falls under Amber category). This readiness level indicates that although the organisation is unprepared for the implementation, however, with minor corrective action, the organisation should be able to achieve READY status for the implementation of SPC.

The outcome in Figure 7.5 reflects that the company has yet to achieve the necessary preparedness to implement SPC according to the evaluation criteria

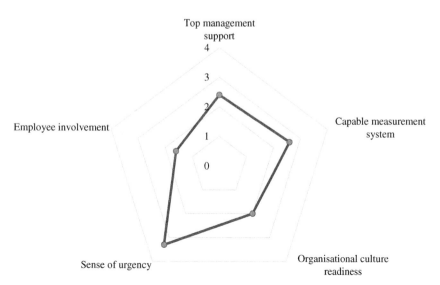

Overall SPC Readiness score

Figure 7.5 Overall SPC readiness score.

of the SPC readiness assessment tool. The analysis of results also revealed that it is not sufficient to only have a sense of urgency, but to also aim for top management support, measurement system capability, and employee involvement in quality management efforts. SPC works best in organisations that are prepared to empower employees and sufficiently train them (Deming 1986).

Readiness is just the beginning of the implementation process! The most critical phase is the implementation process which is often challenging. The managers should have an implementation strategy to ensure that the SPC is not just another fad in the company, but also a technique that can be continuously applied in the business. The next chapter will provide an in-depth understanding of implementing SPC using a roadmap of a food company.

7.8 Summary

- SPC Readiness Self-assessment Tool enables managers to invest in implementing SPC convincingly.
- Food organisations struggle to adopt SPC because there is high resistance to change and lack of guidance to implement the SPC techniques.
- Organisational readiness theory posits that readiness plays a critical role in reducing resistance to SPC adoption.
- SPC Readiness Self-assessment Tool is based on five fundamental readiness factors that are top management support, capable measurement system, organisational culture, sense of urgency, employee involvement.
- SPC Readiness Self-assessment Tool provides a starting point and serves as a checklist for food practitioners to ensure the preparedness of their organisation before beginning the SPC journey. It may also help quality managers to formulate strategies that will foster SPC's long-term use in the company.

8

Critical Aspects in SPC Implementation Process

8.1 Introduction

This chapter presents the principal aspects of the implementation process in the food industry. The managers and Statistical Process Control (SPC) leaders should understand the critical aspects of the implementation process, which consist of:

- effect of company size and commodities
- SPC leader
- critical success factors (CSFs)
- barriers
- performance measurement

This chapter provided the opportunity to view the differences on the impact of SPC implementation compared to the company that did not implement SPC on the operational performances.

8.2 Key Findings from an Empirical Study in the UK Food Manufacturing Industry

Area. England, Scotland, Wales, and Northern Ireland (Refer to Figure 8.1)

The respondents. Directors, Quality Managers, Production Managers, CI (Continuous Improvement) Managers, General Managers, Six Sigma Black Belt and Six Sigma Green Belt.

The results:

- 45% of the respondents implemented SPC in their current company.

Statistical Process Control for the Food Industry: A Guide for Practitioners and Managers, First Edition.
Sarina Abdul Halim Lim and Jiju Antony.
© 2019 John Wiley & Sons Ltd. Published 2019 by John Wiley & Sons Ltd.

Figure 8.1 Type and location of sample food companies in the UK.

Size of a food company and the adoption of SPC in the business: Refer Figure 8.2

- 55.9% categorised as large, 27.11% as medium, and 16.95% as small companies.
- Among the respondents that had applied SPC, 3% were from small, 14% from medium and 29% from large companies (Figure 8.2).

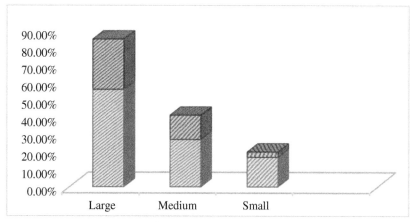

Figure 8.2 Size of company and SPC adoption.

- There is statistical evidence that company size has a significant impact on the adoption of SPC (Chi-square, p-value = 0.011 < 0.05).
- SPC companies have been using the technique for about nine years on average, with a range of 2–15 years. Companies that had applied SPC for more than 10 years were mostly large multinational companies.
- In the food industry, the size of a company influences the adoption of SPC, potentially due to different levels of the quality maturity depicted by the respective size of the company.
- The prominent reason restricting small organisations from adopting SPC is lack of resources – particularly time, budget and personnel (Dora et al. 2013a). This lack of resources may force small food companies to prioritise their quality techniques, thus resulting in more food safety activities being practiced instead of advanced process control techniques such as SPC, due to their obligation to comply with food laws and regulations. Hazard Analysis Critical Control Point (HACCP) is one of the major quality certifications used by the food manufacturing companies (FMCs) for the food safety purposes. However, SPC, which operates almost in a similar manner, is less likely to be applied in the food industry. This is also true for medium-sized food companies, although they are more flexible, compared to small and large companies, when it comes to adopting new techniques.

Type of commodities affected the adoption of SPC in the food industry

- There is statistical evidence that different type of commodities has a significant impact on the adoption of SPC (Chi-square, p-value = 0.011 < 0.05).

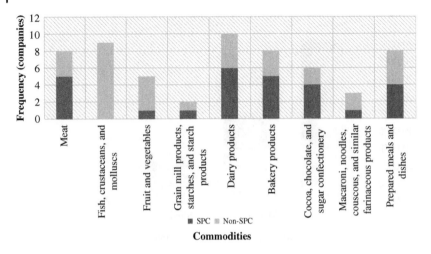

Figure 8.3 Type of commodities.

- Figure 8.3 illustrates the type of company (SPC or non-SPC) according to the food commodities, SPC implementation in companies processing fresh products, such as fish, crustaceans, molluscs, fruit, and vegetables, significantly lagging behind other commodities.
- SPC adoption is slow in the food industry, bearing in mind the fact that the big wave of SPC implementation in western manufacturing companies began 35 years ago.
- Type of company (based on main products/commodities manufactured by the company) has a significant impact on the adoption of SPC.
- It is largely due to the different levels of complexity involved in manufacturing the respective type of products, the shelf-life of the product and the strictness/enforcement of food law to a certain type of food commodities.
- For instance, fresh food products typically involve fewer processes, which give the impression to quality managers that such processes do not require advanced techniques as the operational design centres on sanitation and food safety, and higher production speeds through automation and product traceability (Lamikanra 2002).

8.3 CSF of SPC Implementation

The idea that there are a few factors that can ascertain which decisions ensure the success of a company was introduced by Daniel (1961). Later on, Rockart (1979) elaborated on the idea of CSFs where he defines CSFs as the limited number of key areas where satisfactory results will ensure successful competitive performance for the individual, department, or organisation.

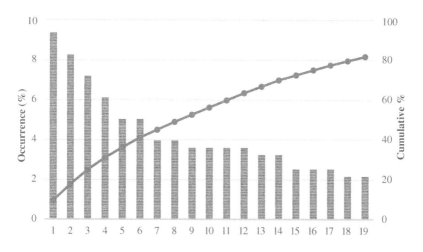

1. Top management commitment
2. Training
3. Measurement system
4. Control chart application
5. Teamwork/Implementation team
6. Cultural change
7. Identification of critical quality characteristics
8. Data management and SPC software
9. Process prioritization
10. Pilot study
11. Data requirement
12. Feedback and responsiveness
13. CI culture
14. Process description
15. Program planning
16. Documentation
17. SPC facilitators
18. Customer satisfaction orientation
19. Employee empowerment

Figure 8.4 Pareto analysis of CSFs in SPC implementation.

It is imperative to consider theoretical components in the existing SPC implementation frameworks developed based on the CSFs listed in the previous empirical studies (Noskievičová 2010; Kumar and Motwani 1996; Does and Trip 1997; Dogdu, Santos, and Dougherty 1997; Krumwiede and Sheu 1996; Antony and Taner 2003). Halim Lim et al. (2017) stated 19 general SPC implementation CSFs were identified regardless of the industry, where the CSFs were analysed using Pareto analysis in Figure 8.4.

Using Pareto analysis as above, the managers are easily able to prioritise the CSFs they need to focus and to plan on a successful SPC implementation strategically. Figure 8.4 depicts 80%, top management commitment and training sessions are two critical issues in assuring the success of SPC in a company. However, in practice, each factor has different significance in each company, and although the importance is understood, it does not mean that the frequency of implementation will follow the same pattern.

8.4   Gap Between the Importance of SPC and the Frequency of Actual Practice

The empirical study in the UK food industry identified real practices example of the gap between the importance of the CSFs the practitioners perceived and the seriousness of its implementation in the industry. The SPC users were asked to rate the 'importance' and 'practice' of CSFs of SPC implementation according to their experience in implementing SPC, where the importance and the frequency of each factor practised were asked to be scored using a Likert scale.

Importance. The question involved here is how critical for the company to apply SPC? Typically for the managers to answer this question, they have to have a clear view on their current process performance and aware the existence of SPC and its mechanism in process control initiative.

Practice. How much have we implemented SPC? Although the managers are aware of SPC and critical in the business, it is not necessarily that the company adopts the technique as frequent as its importance to the business. This may due to several barriers to SPC implementation, such as lack of sufficient training, resistance to change, lack of management support, and other factors, which are discussed further in Section 8.5 of this chapter.

The idea of determining a set of CSFs for managers to prioritise was introduced by Rockart (1979). CSFs are defined as the limited number of areas that are suggested to result in improved competitive performance, if they are satisfactorily implemented (Rockart 1979).

Based on Table 8.1, top management commitment was determined as the most important factor among the CSFs for SPC implementation, while project management received the lowest mean value of importance. There are gaps between the 'importance' of the factors and the degree of implementation (practice), where 'importance' was found to have a higher mean score for every CSF listed.

- SPC implementation will have a higher potential to fail and to be 'short-lived' in a company when the top management show no support towards the SPC adoption in the organisation.
- The level of support by top management differs for each company. Convinced top management ensured resources such as time, training, and employees were made available.
- The commitment of top management in a company is exemplary and reflects the seriousness of the top management towards the adoption.

Table 8.1 The rank of CSFs according to its importance and frequency in practice.

Factors	Importance	Practice
Top management commitment	1	1
Reliable measurement system	2	6
Understanding of statistical thinking	3	7
Leadership	4	2
Continuous training sessions	5	8
Empowerment	6	5
Availability of SPC expertise	7	9
Prioritisation of process	8	3
Project management	9	4

- As there is still confusion between top management and leadership roles, Kotter (2008a) differentiates between the two by explaining that management produces consistency, while leadership produces movement.
- Among the supports which that top management can portray in the SPC implementation, are:
  - allocate sufficient financial support;
  - offer training sessions to the selected staff and follow some of the SPC training sessions;
  - allocate a sufficient number of staff;
  - nominate an SPC leader;
  - offer employees empowerment; and
  - provide a reward and recognition system.

As the food industry is known for its challenging nature to accept new management technology, a changing agent that leads towards implementation should be nominated. The empirical study revealed that an SPC leader is responsible for implementing and strategically planning on the sustainment of SPC in the company. This SPC leader is given the authority to make SPC implementation related decisions and must be diligent, enthusiastic and passionate about SPC implementation.

It is useful for top management to understand who is commonly responsible for leading and spearheading SPC implementation in the food industry (Figure 8.5). The posts of SPC leaders in an organisation are as follow (Abdul Halim Lim et al. 2017):

- Most common SPC leader in the food company are quality managers (20.34%) and technical managers (6.78%) to manage and lead their SPC programmes.

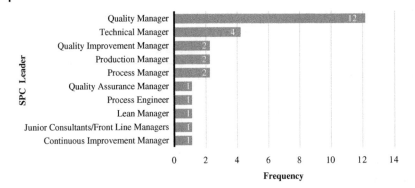

Figure 8.5 Common SPC leader in the food companies.

- Quality managers typically were trusted with the responsibility for managing all quality issues in the company, as they are expected to have more knowledge and experience on quality compared to other personnel, despite the complexity of the food processes (Hubbard 2003).
- The SPC leader is responsible for motivating team members, reducing the blame cultures, assigning tasks, guiding employees to use the technique, securing sufficient resources and making sure the project is delivered within the expected timeline.
- The SPC leader can be viewed as a change agent in the organisation.
- Planning SPC training programme is one of the main tasks of the SPC leader.

8.5 Common Barriers to SPC Implementation

The top three barriers discussed in the literature are the resistance to change, lack of sufficient statistical knowledge, and deficiency of management support. More details on the barriers to SPC implementation in the food industry are listed in the Table 8.2 and the details are as follows:

Resistance to Change

- Current food organisations have not fully accepted the need for CI techniques
- Fear of failure
- Complacency with current performance

Lack of Statistical Knowledge

- They are unfamiliar with the use of advanced statistical techniques.
- Decision-making based on data is not a customary practice in the food industry.

- SPC is perceived as being too advanced for the food industry.
- Multivariate control chart application is too challenging for the shop floor employees to handle.

Lack of Management Support

- Resistance to provide sufficient resources;
- Lack of management awareness on SPC;
- Improvement project activities are not of the highest priority;
- Managing directors do not appreciate the value of SPC; and
- Lack of encouragement for employee involvement.

Poor Measurement System

- Lack of awareness towards the importance of capable measurement system;
- Lack of maintenance;
- Lack of training to measure; and
- Lack of standard procedure to measure.

Lack of Practical Guidelines

- There is no practical manual for food manufacturers to initiate SPC implementation.
- Lack of manual on choosing and using quality tools.

Lack of Employee Empowerment

- Most of the food companies do not welcome suggestions and opinions from employees for quality improvement purposes.
- No standard operating procedure for the employees to investigate any issues which occur.

Lack of Trained Employees

- A study in a high-volume production facility that applied extremely rigorous SPC abandons the technique due to lack of in-house expertise.
- Many statistical techniques are perceived as too advanced for untrained staff in the food industry.
- Lack of knowledge about the tools.

Lack of Experience

- Lack of experience in using quality tools obstructs quality improvement initiatives in food companies.
- The sense of quality of the operators is still low.

Table 8.2 Barriers towards the SPC implementation.

Barriers	Rank
Insufficient training sessions on SPC implementation	1
Employees lack awareness of SPC and its benefits	2
Lack of top management support	3
Poor measurement system	4
Lack of a data collection system	5
Lack of experience in quality improvement tools/techniques/methods	6
Lack of knowledge for SPC implementation	7
Lack of ability to apply SPC in the real world	8
Lack of systematic and practical guidelines for SPC implementation	9
Resistance to accepting SPC as a process improvement technique	10
Lack of employee empowerment	11

Costly Technique

- SPC is perceived as a luxury approach due to training and software requirements for its application

8.6 Process Performance Measurement

The success of an SPC implementation has a close link to process performance measurement. The success of SPC implementation is crucial for its continuance where process performance can be viewed as evidence. Companies that have applied SPC were measured by their process performance on product quality and operational criteria, rather than on business performance criteria such as customer satisfaction and customer loyalty. This study accentuates the poor process performance measurement, especially the lack of process capability indices' application (e.g. Cp/Cpk and Pp/Ppk) as process performance measurement. The encouraging results obtained from the SPC users compared to non-SPC companies shows that SPC has an advantage in operational performance measures (e.g. waste reduction, defect rates, rework rates). The respondents were also required to rate the process improvement level achieved by their company in Table 8.3, by using a Likert scale (1 = Very poor, 2 = Poor, 3 = Fair, 4 = Good, 5 = Excellent).

These results reveal that the performance metrics commonly used in the food companies were customer satisfaction (64.41%) and customer complaints (62.71%). Most respondents agreed that waste reduction is the most significant

Table 8.3 Process performance.

Process performance measurement	SPC companies	Non-SPC companies	Mann-Whitney U test (Asymp. Sig)
Waste reduction (Over-fill/giveaway/under-fill)	4.64	3.32	0.000*
Product consistency	4.32	3.67	0.004*
Customer complaints reduction	4.24	3.48	0.000*
Competitive advantage	4.14	3.79	0.273
Defects percentages reduction	4.12	3.18	0.001*
Productivity improvement	4.09	3.43	0.002*
Rework percentages	4.08	3.20	0.002*
Company image	4.06	3.92	0.276
Quality awareness	4.05	3.53	0.044*
Customer loyalty	3.94	3.90	0.975
Process cycle time	3.95	3.51	0.052
Cost of quality	3.90	3.36	0.054
Customer satisfaction	3.52	3.34	0.180
Pp/Ppk*	4.27	N/a	N/a
Cp/Cpk*	4.17	N/a	N/a

N/a, Not available; Cpk/Cpk and Pp/Ppk not relevant to non-SPC companies.

advantage gained from SPC implementation, followed by improvements in product consistency. 'Under-filling' is a crucial issue in food products as it relates to consumer trust, and breaching this measurement would lead to customer complaints and penalties for breaching food regulations (e.g. Weight and Measures Act 1979). Hence, the most typical strategy for overcoming such a problem is by exceeding the target volume (over-filling), which leads to wastage of raw materials.

Table 8.3 also demonstrates that SPC companies have better process performance scores for all performance metrics compared to the non-SPC companies. Through Mann-U Whitney test, there are significant differences between SPC and non-SPC companies about waste, product consistency, customer complaints, defect rates, productivity, rework percentages, and quality awareness.

The gap analysis was not carried out for any process capability index (Cp, Cpk, Pp, Ppk) as the pre-requisite to carry out process capability analysis is that the process must be statistically stable, and this cannot be confirmed for non-SPC companies (Brannstrom-Stenberg and Deleryd 1999; Castagliola and Vännman (2007); Ittner and Larcker 1997; Montgomery 2012).

Most of the food companies measured waste, scrap and productivity (yield or throughput) as the performance measurement of their processes. The productivity is calculated differently in each company: either by:

(1) taking the total number of good products; or
(2) integrating other factors such as reworks, energy and raw material.

Theoretically, productivity has been classified to total factor productivity, partial factor productivity and multifactor productivity, which each involved different factors for the calculation.

8.7 Summary

- This chapter comprises SPC's application in the UK food industry and emphasised on the critical dimensions, such as CSFs, barriers, the SPC leader, challenges and the impact of SPC on process performance measurement. An empirical study in the UK food industry is used to provide the real practice information with regards to the implementation process and assist by providing an example from an empirical study in the UK food industry.
- The adoption of SPC was highly influenced by the size of the company, where large companies are more capable of investing in training and hiring facilitator to aid their employees to use SPC, compared to the smaller companies.
- The high resistance to change, lack of training related to quality improvement and a shortage of statistical knowledge and skills has acted as the constraints to the SPC implementation in this sector, where lack of training is found to be the most common barriers.
- In order to gain successful SPC implementation, the study confirms the critical factors are; top management commitment, effective training programme and reliable measurement system.
- Sufficient training reduces the reluctance to adopt SPC and enables the food industry personnel to implement a successful SPC technique.
- Availability of SPC leader is found to be crucial and may sometimes view as the change agent, not only to manage the pilot project but also to lead the deployment of SPC in the company under the food quality management. Compared to non-SPC companies, SPC companies were observed to have higher performance levels, which is especially significant in terms of waste reduction, product consistency, customer complaints, defect rates, productivity and rework percentages.
- The evidence is now emerging to show that SPC provides benefits to the food manufacturing industry (FMI), in a similar fashion to Deming's chain reaction model. The Deming chain commonly starts with process variability reduction and ends with the companies surviving, staying in business and improving the ability to return on business investment (Deming 1986).

9

Roadmap for the Deployment of SPC

9.1 A Cookbook Approach

The mechanism of Statistical Process Control (SPC) is simple but effective and powerful for quality control. Thus, it will support quality improvement effort to a great extent if it is applied well. The critical quality parameters of the food products are assessed after comparing the measurements or attributes of the quality factor with the desired target value. The corrective actions need to readjust, decrease, or eliminate the differences if deviations of the value are higher than the acceptable control limit. For instance, food manufacturing factories tend to be hectic. Hence, potential improvements are often ignored or overlooked as there is no responsible person to identify and improve the process. Therefore, the mechanism in SPC allows food businesses to observe analytically what are the processes involved and identify the quality of the process.

Nevertheless, SPC implementation involves data collection and chart filing. Besides this, it also requires a systematic strategy for its implementation. A considerable amount of time and effort will be wasted by seeking cooperation from the employees or redoing tasks if they were conducted incorrectly. The SPC implementation roadmap contains five phases towards successful sustainability of SPC implementation (Lim et al. 2015). Nevertheless, users should be flexible in order to adopt the activities, tools, and methods according to the capacity and capability of the company. This chapter guides the managers and engineers to observe closely and follow a step-by-step process to implement SPC successfully in the food business as depicted in Figure 9.1.

9.2 Phase Awareness: Sell the Program

An awareness of SPC marks a formal start and is considered as the appetiser of the SPC deployment effort in the company. The most crucial step is to initiate a technique regardless of how daunting the technique is. In the awareness

Statistical Process Control for the Food Industry: A Guide for Practitioners and Managers, First Edition.
Sarina Abdul Halim Lim and Jiju Antony.
© 2019 John Wiley & Sons Ltd. Published 2019 by John Wiley & Sons Ltd.

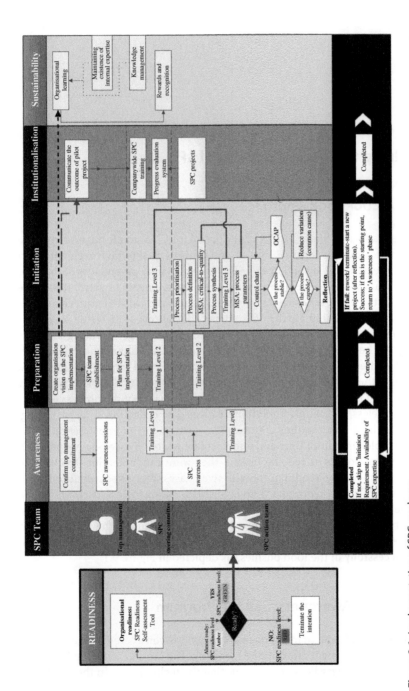

Figure 9.1 Implementation of SPC roadmap.

phase, the principal purpose is to educate and introduce staff and management of the organisation on the reasons of SPC application in current practice, the potential challenges and benefits of such implementation. Apart from that, it also serves to develop a sense of urgency and create values for SPC application in the company and to gain support from the top management.

9.2.1 Step 1: Top to Bottom

Once the food company implements the SPC readiness assessment, the current state of process management is identified. Subsequently, it also indicates the firm has committed top management supporting SPC. The commitment from top management and leaders in the company needs to be confirmed at the preliminary stage of SPC implementation. In general, the top management displays their interest in implementing SPC at the initial phase. Nevertheless, such passion and interest deteriorate throughout the implementation process as most of them are expecting immediate results from the implementation process. Thus, the commitment step is critical, as many food companies have failed in their attempt to implement SPC due to the lack of commitment and support from the top management or lack of drive from the leadership towards the initiative(Lim, Antony, and Arshed 2016) .

The activities suggested in this step are:

- Top management shows support by acquiring knowledge on SPC (i.e. attending the awareness session, training on quality tools and techniques).
- Senior management needs to be aware of and acknowledge the current true performance of the organisation by determining the quality costs.
- Communicate the scope, objectives and requirement of SPC implementation from top to bottom approach.
- Top management is supportive instead of being autocratic. Promote employee involvement in quality improvement activities by authorising process ownership to employees.
- Top management should ensure and confirm that there is no potential change in the leadership of the company.
- Top management is readily able to continuously evaluate the progress of the project and process performance related to SPC.
- Appoint an SPC leader to plan, lead and manage the SPC deployment in the company.

Compared to the requirement for other quality management programmes (e.g. Six Sigma, Hazard Analysis Critical Control Point (HACCP), Good Manufacturing Practice (GMP), Lean), there is not much work need to be done for implementing SPC programmes in the business. Nevertheless, it is crucial for the management to clearly understand the correct idea of SPC implementation. In most cases, SPC failures are primarily due to a false understanding of SPC's purpose and intended outcomes, often by senior management. Therefore, theoretically, the senior management is committed to the implementation. In fact, practically, they are evading direct involvement by delegating the responsibility to their subordinates. According to Dale and Shaw (1989)'s survey for Ford Motor Company, the senior managers are not attending SPC training for several reasons. The employees are incapable of making changes in the company and also have to deal with the accumulated workload during their absence after returning from the SPC training.

Is it a strict rule that SPC implementation cannot occur without top management support? Would implementation still be successful if it is initiated by using the bottom-to-top approach?

- In theory, yes, provided that the implementation starts from a 'critical' process, which subsequently be explained in the 'Initiation' phase, specifically at the Process Prioritisation step. Nevertheless, from the author's experience in real practice, there is hardly evidence of successful story of companywide SPC implementation without top management buy-in.

The competency level of the employees affects the SPC implementation success. Hence, the selection of top talent team members, especially the leader, is crucial (Davie and Ryan 2005; Hersleth and Bjerke 2001). The SPC leader should at least acquires several skills, such as a being logical and analytical, perseverance, excellent project management skills, and zeal in the use of SPC tools. The primary reason is that top talent is a significant consideration during the implementation process. As such, better outcomes can be achieved as talented people are capable of leading and passing on knowledge to others in the company (Snee and Hoerl 2003).

SMEs have the advantage of having faster communication across the business due to their flat layer structure and less functional hierarchy (Maneesh 2010). Thus, a **communication plan** should be developed for all senior management and employees to be aware of the quality improvement efforts and to understand the reason for the implementation. The top management may inform the employees of their intention of SPC adoption through emails, bulletin board, company's web page, or meetings. This step is considered complete when the top management is supportive to commit to SPC and understand their role towards a successful SPC implementation and intention to adopt SPC.

9.2.2 Step 2: SPC Awareness Sessions

This step is viewed as the formal start of education about SPC in the company, i.e. an awareness meeting for the senior management of the company. The objectives of the awareness sessions may be equivalent to the training sessions (except it is much shorter in time, and requires less technical materials). The general objectives are:

- to familiarise the senior management with the principal philosophy of SPC;
- to build a positive impression with respect to SPC adoption in the company; and
- to emphasise the expected commitment and required for the SPC implementation to be successful.

The involvement of top management in the awareness session is to convince the employees on the adoption of SPC. Such awareness sessions will secure senior management commitment and faith in the initiative. Thus, it is important to start SPC awareness session at the top of the organisation and be passed down (employees training) through the organisation hierarchy to secure senior management commitment for such implementation.

In the awareness session, the information below must be communicated:

- The linkage of statistical thinking in the process management practice
- Benefits of shifting from detection to prevention approach.
- SPC is a means to move from fire-fighting culture to process improvement.
- SPC requires changes of management style with respect to the delegation of tasks and employee empowerment.
- SPC is a technique used to establish process capabilities and the importance of such metrics is used as the process performance assessment.
- SPC is a technique to recognise, quantify, reduce and control variation.
- SPC is linked to food quality management strategy.

9.2.3 Step 3: SPC Training

It is crucial that everyone in the company is not only aware of the existence of SPC, but also understands clearly the importance of SPC and how it can be advantageous to the employees and subsequently for the company. Similar to a top management awareness session, at this stage, SPC should be introduced with emphasis on definitions, requirements, and benefits. In the food industry, training for quality were highly sought after, (based on the result in SPC case studies) with regards to food safety, which is encouraged to include in the

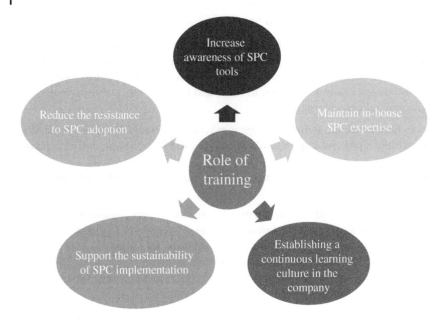

Figure 9.2 Role of SPC training.

SPC module (for Level 1) within the training session or other training programs under food quality management.

The current training session mainly focuses on the technical aspect (control chart construction, sampling, interpretation of the statistical results), neglecting the managerial aspects, which often causes the failure of SPC implementation (Hoerl 1995). The most ineffective approach is to provide all the information in one training session. However, to provide training at each step along the implementation process will cost the company extra time and money. The purpose of SPC training (Figure 9.2) should be clear and well-communicated to the employees.

Ensuring the module of the training matches the level of employees' knowledge is essential in the food industry as the workforce were reported to have low level of knowledge and statistical skills. A survey distributed to the employees in a company will always reveal special skills, knowledge, interests, and motivations of employees and this information could be used to enrich the role of employees in SPC. In order to increase its effectiveness and efficiently use the resources (time, money), the level of SPC training depicted in Figure 9.3 is divided into three levels.

For smaller food companies, they were suggested to collaborate with other organisations/business, customers or government bodies or academics institution for training and support the initial phase of the adoption as the most prevalent resource constraint is financial (Dora et al. 2013a).

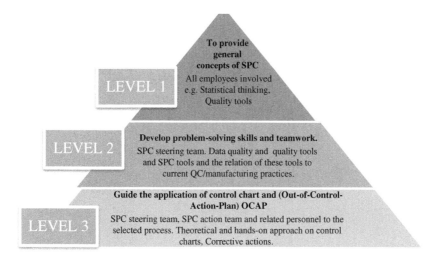

Figure 9.3 SPC training holistic program.

Food companies are also suggested to seek external advice from consultation companies or academic institutions. Local universities are able to facilitate food companies in several ways to embark on their CI journey such as trainings (e.g. statistics and its applications), principal of SPC, tools and techniques of CI; student internship work on the SPC or Six Sigma project supported by an academic mentor, work with the Knowledge Transfer Programme.

9.3 Phase Preparation

Based on the first findings in the literature, successful implementation requires cautious preparation (Oakland and Tanner 2007). The key important points relating to the efforts of preparing for the implementation process are shown in Figure 9.4.

9.3.1 Step 4: Corporate SPC Vision Create/Creating a SPC Corporate Vision

Top management needs to create and clearly communicate the vision and mission statements for SPC implementation. SPC should be linked with the company's food quality management (FQM) system to improve food quality and maintain food safety (Kolesar 1993; Stuart, Mullins, and Drew 1996; Vanderspiegel et al. 2005). It is the top management responsibility to draw the direction for SPC deployment in the company complete with a clear target, people involved, time and budget allocation for the deployment.

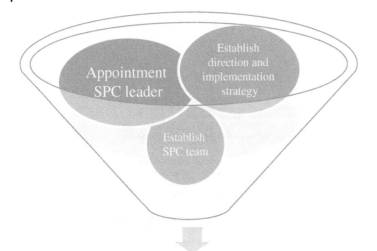

Components for preparing on the SPC
adoption in the company

Figure 9.4 Preparation phase.

9.3.2   Step 5: SPC Team Establishment

Appointing an SPC leader is the first step in developing the SPC team. Thus, it is the obligation of top management to appoint an SPC leader who has a great passion for quality improvement with a sense of urgency in relation to the initiation of SPC (Morgan 2006).

Some roles of the SPC leader:

- A change agent.
- Chair the team meeting.
- Issue instructions required to complete the project.
- Assign tasks to the team members.
- Maintain a continuous application of SPC.
- Develop a strategic plan for a companywide SPC deployment and sustainability.

Leaders must have tte following attitude:

- Positive attitude;
- Initiative–willingness to dig in and get started;
- Ambitions–always broadening view, developing new skills, and willingness to take a risk;

- Self-confident–a competitor, one who gets the job done;
- Courage and willingness to train a successor;
- Flexible–not set in his ways;
- Resilient–ability to bounce back;
- Stamina and mental attitude to cope with endless streams of stress;
- Ability to judge people and how to develop people;
- Goal setter–long range plans including budgets and deadlines, collaborator;
- Imaginative, creative, with great self-discipline.

One of the SPC leader's responsibilities is to establish an SPC team. Teamwork is an important element underlying SPC philosophy (Deming 1986). The development of a team is a critical obligation for SPC leaders and top management to select the team members and equip them with knowledge, authority, and commitment. The team establishment depends on the size of the company as a small company may consist of the top management team and SPC implementation team (i.e. integration of SPC steering team and action team). Thus, large companies should be able to develop a bigger team. Furthermore, the multi-disciplinary team works well in expanding SPC due to its ability to capitalise on the knowledge diversity of the team members, to encourage collaboration for better problem solving, innovative decisions and to the extent of engagement in the implementation of proposed solutions. Chapter 6 provides further guidelines for team formation.

9.3.3 Step 6: Develop Strategic Plans for the SPC Implementation

SPC in the food industry involves a complex process and raw materials, which requires people to work together and often under time pressure. Besides, such a complex process also requires an efficient and effective process for products that have a tight margin. Meanwhile, it also requires attention to detail and careful planning for the implementation to be a success (Dora et al. 2013a,b). Thus, the SPC steering team has the responsibility to commence the introduction, development, and planning of the implementation process (Does and Trip 1997).

This step formulates SPC strategies in line with the vision and mission set up by the top management. Such planning should cover several aspects such as people, time, tools, training, activities, and resources for the pilot projects (Clute 2008). This step is to ensure that the implementation of SPC can be operated within the company and availability of facilities and resources. The targets of this strategic plan are:

- to ease the SPC adoption in the organization;
- to guide and manage the implementation process;
- to ensure the right people and resources are involved at the right time;

- to increase the success of SPC implementation; and
- to convince the top management as the blueprint of their investment is demonstrated in the plan.

The food companies may view the element of an SPC implementation strategic plan as guided by the SPC Implementation Roadmap in this book and adopt it in the respective companies.

9.4 Phase Initiation

The pilot project is crucial when it comes to providing clear and objective evidence on the benefits of SPC implementation to the company and subsequently to capture the attention of top management team. Typically, a pilot project can take from three months to more than a year, depending on the complexity and size of the process (Does and Trip 1997). If this is the starting point of the implementation, the positive outcome should be communicated to the top management (return to phase A). The company-wide institution of SPC is not possible without top management support and commitment.

9.4.1 Step 7: Process Prioritisation

Initial control charts should be implemented for the product characteristics or processes perceived to be crucial or critical to the business. Sources such as production reports, failure cost, and customer complaints can assist in identifying the problem areas and selecting one area to focus. Identification of potential project brings potential improvement in a process that will result in a significant breakthrough.

Typically, the team considers both 'one factor' (number of defects) and 'multiple-criteria's' to choose a good initiation project in the food industry. Therefore, a set of criteria must be developed and should be based on realistic metrics that are easily or readily measurable. The creation of the criteria should also focus on the critical-to-quality, critical-to-cost, critical-to-delivery, and critical-to-responsiveness by the food companies. Therefore, the core SPC team may use prioritisation matrix and develop its template according to the respective food businesses to secure the easiness and motivation for prioritisation for the purpose of accommodating the rapid movement in the production site and tolerating with the shortage of statistical skills of the employees in the food industry (e.g. Microsoft Excel). One of other option for multiple-criteria optimisation is by using Analytic Hierarchy Process (AHP).

The success of the pilot project would act as a model for the rest of the company to follow. It is desirable that the finance department is involved from the commencement of the project to guarantee that the cost-benefit analysis is conducted for each SPC project and savings are, in fact, reflected in the bottom-line.

When implementing AHP, one must able to provide sufficient and relevant information to:

- thoroughly represent the problem;
- consider environment surrounding the problem;
- identify the attributes that contribute to the solutions; and
- identify the personnel of the company associated with the problem.

Nevertheless, AHP will become difficult to be implemented if there is insufficient background information of the case.

9.4.2 Step 8: Process Description

During this step, the SPC team should examine the selected project by mapping the project boundaries. The team members map the process in detail by numbering the process steps coherently following the real situation of the process (Rungtusanatham, Anderson, and Dooley 1997). Similar to HACCP guidelines, this step can be conducted by using process flowchart, process map or Value Stream Mapping (Hurst and Harris 2013).

Several approaches to carry out process prioritisation:

- Pareto analysis (singular criteria/requirement)
- Prioritisation matrix (multi-criteria)
- QFD (Quality Function Deployment) and AHP (Analytic hierarchy process) (multi-criteria)

It is advisable to assign more than one team member for mapping the process in the manufacturing plant to avoid biases and to improve accurateness. This step is completed when the selected process is defined in terms of its performance, process description forms with process step numbers and names, key sub-processes, and other information relevant to the objective of the project. Apart from that, the team also discovers the key processes that influence the critical quality parameter and measures the defects and waste currently generated relative to those processes during this step. Thus, in this step, some improvement opportunity can be detected by comparing different work methods, different operators, different shifts and engineering information (Does and Trip 1997). Moreover, other quality tools that can be applied include group voting, nominal group techniques, Value Stream Mapping and multi-vari charts.

9.4.3   Step 9: Process Synthesis

This step identifies critical process parameters and describes the main problems related to their effects (the problems should be process related). Food companies face difficulties with identifying critical process parameters on the scientific and quantitative basis (Luning and Marcelis 2006).

Some of the processes in the food industry are complex due to the characteristics of the ease of deterioration, and the end product of one method of food processing can be the raw-material for other products. The critical parameters of the product should be investigated by the team. If the team has a long history with the product, the experience of the people involved may provide a big help in the brainstorming session to identify 'what are the key factors/parameters which impacted on the quality of the selected process?'. Up until now, the step is very similar to any conventional method of using experience in decision-making. Decision-making based on experience has a major drawback in terms of its poor evidence in statistical analysis.

It is noteworthy to highlight that there is a risk that the team might jump to conclusions after detecting several possible causes of the problem at this stage.

In this step, the authors suggest the managers may invite the more experienced employees with the process to brainstorm their ideas through several session of cause–effect analysis. At this point the team will have several potential factors that could have an effect on the quality of the process. If there are too many cause–effect factors to be assessed (e.g. more than 100), it is suggested to prioritise and to choose the most important critical and frequently effected or the relations need to be prioritised using Pareto analysis (refer Chapter 5) or multi-voting approach (each of the team members will rank the factors based on criticality). Design of Experiment (DOE) is one of the effective techniques used to identify the critical parameters in a process, which always take place after several potential factors identified from the brainstorming session. (Dalgiç, Vardin, and BelibaÄŸli 2011; Hung and Sung 2011). The output of this step is the SPC team has identified the critical point at which to plant the control chart application, and its critical parameters were identified. It is strongly suggested that the control parameters of the process are measurable and can be monitored based on good quality of data.

9.4.4   Step 10: Measurement System Analysis (MSA)

The main limitations of current FQM practices are poor relevant monitoring systems, lack of proper equipment and incorrect choice of measuring equipment. The capability of the measurement system is assessed by identifying the variability of gauges or instrument. Data are required in the food companies for many critical reasons including for food safety, product quality, legal requirement, customer service, cost control, and actionable cost. In Measurement System Analysis (MSA), the application of Gage Reproducibility and Repeatability (GR&R) views variability from the perspective of the machine and variability of people in using the machine itself, respectively (Hung and Sung 2011; Srikaeo, Furst, and Ashton 2005). Most manufacturing companies follow the Automotive Industry Action Group (AIAG) manual rule of thumb:

The company may require re-calibration of the equipment/machines, preventive maintenance, update to the latest model of manufactured machines and increased training of operators as corrective actions for incapable measurement system (Kovach and Cho 2011; Srikaeo, Furst, and Ashton 2005). Typically, the food companies encounter the issue of having altered or destroyed samples during the testing process and they cannot be retested. Hence, these companies have to be considered by using destructive GR&R experiments. Thus, the key parameters for the GR&R should be operators and machines.

< 10% Acceptable	10% to 30% May be acceptable	>30% Unacceptable

9.4.5   Step 11: Control Chart

This step is the foci of the SPC implementation to understand the process variation and process mean, detect or avoid the out-of-control situation. The next steps are constructing control charts and interpretation of the control chart (Hayes, Scallan, and Wong 1997) (refer to Figure 9.2) once critical process parameters or Critical Points (for HACCP) have been identified.

In terms of sampling methods, the sample size for control chart, 25 or more subgroups or more than a 100 individual readings provide a sufficiently good test for stability (Montgomery 2012). The Operating Characteristic curves are helpful in selecting the sample size. For the frequency of sampling, the typical strategies available are: (i) to take small but frequent samples, or (ii) take large samples but less frequent. The selection process is depicted in Figure 9.7 and the selection of the right control chart is critical to prevent a false alarm signal (Montgomery 2012) (Figure 9.5).

It is also useful to distinguish between Phase I and Phase II methods in the application of control chart (Woodall and Spitzner 2004). Phase I of a control chart is a retrospective analysis where the process data are gathered and analysed all at once. The purposes are to confirm reliability and to monitor future production to determine the state of the (control or not in control) production. After the process has been stabilized, and the process data are steadily represented for the in-control process performance, phase II starts with the

Pre-construction

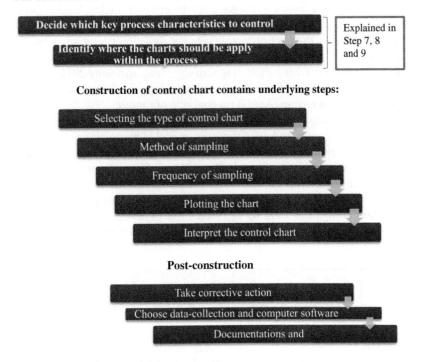

Figure 9.5 Steps for control chart construction.

application of a control chart to monitor the process by comparing the sample stylistic for each successive sample to the control limits. Shewhart's control charts are commonly utilized, since they are easy to construct, interpret, and are effective in detecting the arch and sustained shifts in process parameters and outliers and measurement error (Montgomery 2012).

Nevertheless, in practice, process parameters are commonly unknown or unspecified. For such cases, phase 1 analysis is applied to bring the process in control. Later, phase II control limits are calculated using the set of the data from the 'in control' process (reference data or calibration data).

Shewhart's mean and range chart is identified as the most applied control charts in the food industry. For instance, many food productions that run the small-batch processes use application of short-run SPC charts. As the food industry involves complex processes, it is a good practice to maintain and update the information on the control charts involved:

- Keep the total number of control charts applied in the process.
- Keep records for each type of control chart (attribute or variable control chart).
- Record the place in the process where the control charts were applied.

Therefore, typical SPC program will initiate the attributes control chart, as most of the control charts will be implemented at the end of the production line that can be finished product or semi-finished product. Practically, if the control charts are implemented effectively and new information gained, the application of attribute charts will be reduced whereas $\bar{x}$ and R charts will increase. As more information is provided regarding the process, the control charts will subsequently be applied at the critical parameters of the process that caused nonconformities. Typically, at this point, $\bar{x}$ and R charts will replace the attributes charts applied earlier.

The out-of-control signals can be identified by adopting decision rules for Shewhart control charts, published in West Electric Handbook (1956). Chapter 5 states the other decision rules for control charts. Typically, the employees used simple tools for analysis, such as trend graphs, histogram, Pareto chart, and scatter diagram;. Nevertheless, occasionally a more complicated technique, such as AHP, Taguchi and DOE, requires the knowledge of the experts.

9.4.6 Step 12: Establish Out-of-Control-Action-Plan (OCAP)

It is recommended that the root cause of the problem be investigated, and to solve it by using a standard guideline in the procedure of eliminating the assignable cause (Fortune, Reid, and Miller 2013; Grigg and Walls 2007b). At this point, it is crucial that the top management communicate their official support on the empowerment of the employee in taking corrective action towards the OOC process. The SPC team in the company should develop their own Out-of-Control-Action-Plan (OCAP) based on the environment of the company to accommodate their resources and employees' knowledge and skills to conduct the corrective actions. OCAP is an output-oriented alternative, which is in the form of the flowchart showing a sequence of activities that can prescribe actions to remove special causes (Figure 9.6) (Montgomery 2012).

OCAP is the primary step in driving the food companies to adopt *double-loop learning* through SPC implementation. Senge (2006) explained such an approach to learning is required to achieve organisational learning. Constructing OCAP contributes to a better-organised decision-making process and promoting employee empowerment culture. Apart from that, OCAP becomes a significant knowledge base for the SPC action team members (Hood and Wilson 2001). The operators and engineers that are directly related to the process should be provided direct authority for collecting data, interpreting

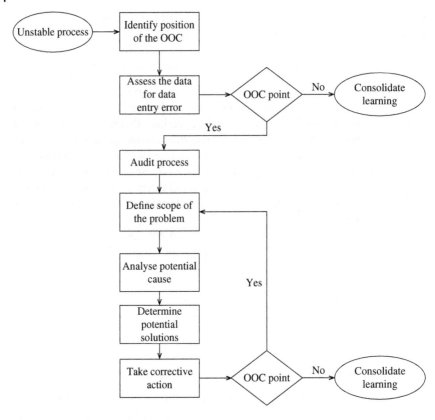

Figure 9.6 Out-of-control action-plan.

and stabilising the charts as they have the knowledge of the process. OCAP is not a static document, therefore it should be updated and revised reflecting on how much the team learned about new information about the process.

Food companies need to be cautious and ensure that food safety and food regulation is not compromised with the change or corrective action taken.

9.4.7 Step 13: Process Capability

Process capability is rarely applied in the food industry as the measurement to assess process performance. As a result, many food companies fail to understand the concept of process variation when process capability analysis criteria have not been implemented after the process stability is achieved.

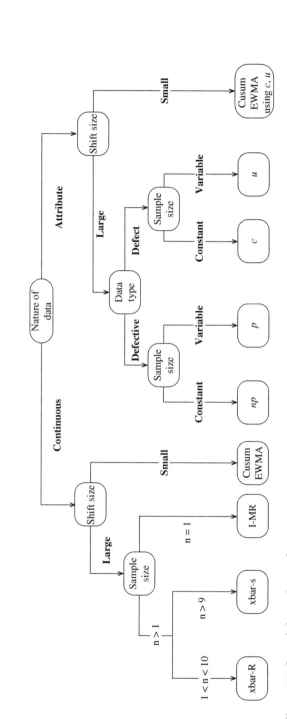

Figure 9.7 Control chart selection flowchart.

The importance of this step (process capability analysis) is to determine whether the process is able to meet customer specifications. For instance, the process capability should be calculated to quantify the ratio between tolerance width and process inherent variation (Cp index) and the effect of this ratio due to the variation and the deviation of the position of the process mean from the target value (Cpk index). Furthermore, the process capability analysis measures the variability of a process based on these assumptions. Apart from that, the process is in the state of statistical control and the data follow a normal distribution (Montgomery 2012). The number of non-conforming products may be predicted and the usage of the histogram may provide the level of statistical control needed since the process is stable (in statistical control) (Does and Trip 1997; Özilgen 1998).

In the food industry, data do not necessarily following a normal distribution, but mostly the non-normal distributed process. There are various approaches to deal with the non-normal data such as data transformation to normal data, an extension of the definitions of the standard capability indices to a non-normal distribution, modification of the capability indices. As such, these approaches can be appropriate for the common families of distribution (Pearson and Johnson families) (Montgomery 2012).

9.4.8   Step 14: Reflection

The pilot project is not considered complete until the target achieved and a team of financial auditors signs off. Reflection of the pilot project is significant to assess the initial SPC implementation in the company, which involves the evaluation of process performance, financial savings, and SPC action team activities (Antony and Taner 2003; Does and Trip 1997). Furthermore, the accounting representative is advised to participate in this process to measure cost benefits from the project. Cost savings gained from the SPC implementation project should be determined to communicate or announce easily the success or failure of the project to the entire company. The result and the official reward for their results should be announced and communicated during the meeting with all SPC steering teams and the SPC action teams.

The most important activity is to assess the feedback, suggestions, critique of the activities and approaches adopted in the project, and to incorporate such information in the next project plan. Therefore, the project stakeholders and all the SPC team members should participate in this particular step. The information in this step should be a valuable source of information for the next SPC projects, which will be conducted by several other SPC action teams. Moreover, the maturity of SPC implementation in the company will be able to be measured through this step.

9.5 Phase Institution: Company-Wide Implementation

This phase is outlining the activities involved in applying SPC to other processes or departments of the company. The company should publicise the outcome of the project, widen the number of participants for training sessions, and promote the opportunities to implement SPC in the non-production departments so that the culture of statistical thinking and CI is embedded within the organisation.

9.5.1 Step 15: Communicate the Success of Initial Project

Communication is an activity of conveying information and knowledge, and it is ranked among the key factors contributing to the success of the process improvement. Awareness and recognition towards SPC implementation are achievable through effective communication of successful SPC projects. For instance, financial savings and other outcomes generated by the pilot project should be communicated throughout the companies. Financial advantages are the effective language to convince the top management towards the implementation of SPC. Apart from that, several communication strategies are available in most of the food companies such as a newsletter, bulletin board, company's webpage, intranet, etc. Critical information should be considered in this step are: the ability to widely celebrate and share the success of pilot projects, the appreciation from top management and the need to share the major challenges and pitfalls during the implementation of the project.

The successful pilot project reduces the resistance of management and employees towards SPC. Besides, it also increases the motivation of SPC implementation within the organisation. In fact, communication should not stop internally and must be extended to the knowledge of the suppliers. Thus, a well-communicated successful improvement provides motivation and incentives to improve the processes and subsequently to make continuous improvement as the core culture of the business.

9.5.2 Step 16: Company-Wide Training

Based on previous empirical studies, the training should offer different levels of training as the employees in the food industry acquire a big range of knowledge level in CI and statistics in particular. Typically, in-house experts lead this step through the SPC implementation plan of the company under the FQM system. SPC training recommends inviting an external trainer and to later build an in-house training to follow up on projects and workshops. The most effective strategy for such training is to start small and to develop a bank of experiences and knowledge (Grigg 1998). Typically, a three-day SPC course is followed within six weeks by a one or two-day workshop (Does and Trip 1997). The training materials should focus on statistical tools, leadership, change of culture, and wider attendance of employees from different types of the department should be encouraged at this point of training sessions (Efstratiadis et al. 2000).

9.5.3   Step 17: Progress Evaluation Systems

The SPC steering team is responsible for continuously monitoring the performance of critical processes. Having good performance measurement induces target areas with the opportunity of improvement, to be identified and has a key role in communication (Oakland and Tanner 2007). This step is to ensure SPC implementation does not stop only at the pilot project, but is continuously applied in other quality improvement projects. In this step, the SPC team should develop a standard procedure for reporting the project, to communicate the good and poor results to the employees, to ensure the owner of the processes are accountable to report on their own process performance, and a monthly review for the on-going projects should be established.

9.6   Phase Sustainability

The sustainability phase accentuates on the efforts to continue reaping the benefits from the implementation of SPC and learns from the previous implementation phases that could be transferred, managed, and reacted across the organisation on a continuous basis. The principal idea behind this phase is to ensure the knowledge and other benefits generated through SPC implementation are sustained on a long-term basis. Such efforts include maintaining the in-house SPC expertise and providing motivation for other employees to implement the technique.

9.6.1   Step 18: Maintenance of In-house Expertise

The results from the empirical studies revealed that the high employee turnover causes difficulties for the food companies to maintain their in-house experts. Sustaining SPC implementation is definitely challenging as the food industry has limited employee expertise in statistical knowledge. SPC implementation is imperative to ensure knowledge transfer within the organisation is actively progressing to increase the number of in-house experts (Davis and Ryan 2005). On the other hand, continuous awareness training session and workshops can assist the company to achieve such objective (Bidder 1990; Hubbard 1999). Thus, knowledge management is arguably critical in such situations to ensure the company develop in-house expertise (Grigg and Walls 2007a). For companies that have not implemented SPC and do not have an SPC expert, an external SPC facilitator should be hired to conduct training sessions and facilitate the company throughout the implementation process.

9.6.2 Step 19: Towards Learning Organisation

The SPC implementation has a role in nurturing learning culture in the company. Senge (2006) suggested that the notion of organisational learning is through systems thinking, team learning, shared vision, individual mastery, and the use of highly sophisticated mental models. Senge (2006) also highlighted the need for organisations to become learners (e.g. single-loop learners and double-loop learners) towards achieving organisational learning. On the other hand, learning organisation recommended characteristics such as open communication without fear or criticism, learning through teamwork, employees' empowerment for making decisions, action and result in focus and wide learning opportunities (Denton 1998). Benchmarking and learning from best-practice of internal and external competitors should continuously keep the company in the momentum for CI (Mann and Adebanjo 1998). Thus, a regular review session should be established monthly for on-going projects, whereas the past performances should be subsequently updated together with new information (Raper et al. 1997).

The five activities stated in this chapter as the key activities building learning organisations are systematic problem solving, trials and experimentation, continuous learning from experiences, transferring knowledge, and objectively assessing the learning process. SPC implementation reflects on the situation of double-loop learning by questioning the adequacy and quality of data, investigation of the process variation, the governing variables to the process, appropriateness of corrective actions through OCAP plan taken in response to the data. Many researchers believed that the benefits of learning organisation towards food companies are that learning becomes a mainstream activity, constant learning leads to continual change and learning facilitates response to change.

9.6.3 Step 20: Reward System

One cause of failure in deploying and sustaining SPC is that the ignorance of the management regarding the fact that the deployment of SPC can lead to unintentional improvements in intrinsic reward. In fact, the reward system should be designed to appreciate and motivate the employees. Through the reward system, the employees are able to show their commitment to quality and seek opportunities to involve in the SPC implementation. Apart from that, such a system also attracts and maintains the people with knowledge and expertise. By doing this, they show the skills and abilities required to achieve the strategic goal of the company to create a better process performance and subsequently superior organisation. Below are the key suggestions for the managers to develop a reward system:

- Identify and communicate with the group of employees that the reward programme will be developed;
- Communicate with the employees on the criteria or performance that will reinforce the company goals;
- Outline the key measurements of the performance based on the individual/team previous achievement;
- Avoid intangible criteria that will lead the system to favouritism;
- Propose appropriate rewards that continuously motivate the employees;
- Communicate clearly the programme to the employees.

9.7 Summary

- The roadmap for SPC deployment in the food industry involved five phases (Awareness, Preparation, Initiation, Institutionalisation, Sustainability).
- The programme should be initiated by selling the technique from top-to-bottom through awareness sessions and effective training sessions.
- SPC leader should be the change agent, and SPC team should be spearheading the SPC deployment in the company, driving the implementation, while, it is the company effort to ensure the processes are in use of statistical control.
- A successful pilot project is essential in feeding the motivation of the employees to involve in SPC implementation and increase top management buy-in. Pilot project should be representative of the most critical process in the business.
- Different levels of training should be planned and strategised according to the different level of employees in the business.
- In order to apply SPC beyond process control activity, corrective action and feedback system must be implemented.
- Sustainability of the SPC programme in the business can be included in organisational learning culture.

10

Case Studies

This chapter disclosed the case studies gathered from research and literature. Each case study is described in brief, focusing on the application of the specific expediting process control approach it illustrates, including the approach to choose pilot projects, the control of key quality of the process attributes, and the application of various type of control charts served for different types of data. This chapter displays how SPC has been successfully applied in several different situations.

The details and situation of the cases are varied, however in general each will provide the background of the cases, the data and suitable type of charts. The charts are interpreted, and interesting points are discussed in the case study. It is not necessarily to understand the calculation and detail calculations to benefit from this book. Implementing SPC in the organisation, it only requires a few number staff to understand the theory and formulae on the calculations of control charts.

10.1 Application of the Control Charts in the Industries

Control charts are typically taught in the classes and mostly when teaching the theory of SPC it is understandable to find the data for the control chart are the easiest to be understood. Theoretically, normality is expected in the food processing data; however, this is rarely the case in the food industry. In the real-world data, neither SPC nor any other technique is the solution for all problems, where other quality tools may be handy in solving the problem. Ensure the data collected relates to the critical quality characteristics for the process, if they fail to do so, there is a potential that the usage of SPC will lead to ineffective corrective action. Processes in the food industry involved complex living and consequently display variability on processes and practices. It is

Statistical Process Control for the Food Industry: A Guide for Practitioners and Managers, First Edition.
Sarina Abdul Halim Lim and Jiju Antony.
© 2019 John Wiley & Sons Ltd. Published 2019 by John Wiley & Sons Ltd.

very rare for the organisation to fully understand and predict what is happening or going to happen in a process.

10.2 Case Study 1 Monitoring Fish Product Packaging (Grigg, Daly, and Stewart, 1998)

10.2.1 Problem Statement

In the food industry, although food safety is the prominent quality criteria, another criterion that has an impact towards the regulation is the control of weights and measures of the products. The weight and measures are critical as failure in conforming so, potentially to cause financial loss. The typical situations in the filling process which relates to the out-of-control situation are underfill and overfill. If it is overweight, the food producers will be faced with loss costs per unit giveaway. If it is underfilled, the food producer has the risk of providing underweight products to the customer, which they could be penalised for violating the regulations weight and measures. The Trading Standards Officer (TSO) tests the sample of packages using the Average System the requirements encapsulated under the 'three rules for packers' (refer to Appendix C).

10.2.2 Processes

Based on study by Grigg et al. (1998), a medium-sized fish producer based in Scotland uses a pre-checkweigher using SPC system outlined by the guideline in the DTI (Department of Trade and Industry) Codes of Practice. The system was designed to be manual and effective, where in order to operate the system, it is not essential for the staff to acquire high statistical knowledge. The system required input from only one staff member to operate the system. However, there are quantifiable cost-benefits in terms of the control of product overfill and the less easily quantified costs of the consequences of product underfill.

10.2.3 Sampling

For the initial study stage, the average fill level of the process ($\bar{\bar{x}}$) and inherent variability fill of the packing level (standard deviation, (s) or ranges (R)) is estimated. This stage is important in establishing the system process mean and variability. Generally, a larger sample size, n, provides better discernment on the differences between groups. Unfortunately, fish are expensive samples; the larger the sample size, the more expensive the data collection is likely to be. A rules of thumb suggests a sample size at the initial stage is appropriate with $n = 4$ or 5 (Montgomery, 2012). The larger the sample size, the chart will be more sensitive to process changes. In this stage, a minimum of 200 packages are collected in the subgroup size of 5 at the interval of 30 minutes, making to the total of 40 subgroups.

In rational subgroup sampling, consecutive products produced are used for testing.

10.2.4 Type of Data

As the data collected in this case is net weight and it is measureable it therefore provides continuous data (refer Table 10.1). The overall mean fill of the packaging is referred to the mean of the 40 subgroups. As the sample size for this case is 5, it is appropriate to apply an Xbar-R chart (refer to selection of control chart in Figure 9.7).

Table 10.1 Net weight data set (gram).

Sample, i	Mean					Sample, i	Mean				
1	364	361	360	361	360	21	354	361	360	372	366
2	360	362	368	361	364	22	374	374	370	367	372
3	357	364	358	361	361	23	376	377	374	364	371
4	364	362	361	367	358	24	365	375	374	370	362
5	351	365	361	367	358	25	364	362	370	367	367
6	356	364	362	360	359	26	377	376	377	362	382
7	358	359	360	367	365	27	354	367	358	366	350
8	365	357	362	368	364	28	363	356	352	360	357
9	357	361	365	361	363	29	369	360	351	353	359
10	362	363	358	362	360	30	369	361	355	365	357
11	366	369	360	363	362	31	361	364	362	361	360
12	367	358	363	362	362	32	371	365	377	372	351
13	357	364	361	362	365	33	360	371	365	364	373
14	369	371	363	362	362	34	365	366	370	365	367
15	360	358	363	362	360	35	357	370	360	364	365
16	367	380	361	348	364	36	358	367	365	361	357
17	352	354	377	362	353	37	358	357	360	370	363
18	376	365	351	367	363	38	357	382	354	361	373
19	366	361	365	363	363	39	370	361	358	372	377
20	369	371	364	367	371	40	371	358	356	358	360

10.2.5   Construction of the Control Chart

In the Code of Practice guidance, the three types of control chart suggested in the guidance are Run chart, Mean and Range control charts, and CUSUM charts. Based on the type of data, Mean chart and Range chart are the most appropriate charts that fit the purpose to monitor the current processes. In order to monitor and control the average value of the key process variable, e.g. package weight, a mean chart is applied. The lower control limit is to detect underfill. On the variability chart, the main control limit concerned is the upper control limit to identify high variation of the process.

Formula to calculate mean and standard deviation of the process fill:

$$\bar{\bar{x}} = \frac{(360 + 363 + \dots 361)}{40} = 363.54$$

$$\bar{s} = \frac{(1.6 + 3.2 + \dots 6.0)}{40} = 5.06$$

$$\bar{R} = \frac{(4 + 8 + \dots 15)}{40} = 12.80$$

10.2.5.1   Determine the Target Level

The process involved is the filling process of the fish cans. The allowable condition for the filling process based on the angle of regulators are: the process able to fill in the can within the target quantity or minimum target quantity. Objectively, only one side of the control limits are critically needed to be controlled. Despite underweight of the packages being of primary legal importance, high giveaway through overfill of the packages is to be avoided in food packing for economic reasons. For the weight variability charts, it is critical to control the upper control limit is critical to prevent it not becoming too high. The lowest value of the limits is highly preferred as the lower value of the variability, the less inconsistent of the process; it is indicating that the more stable process is in the production. The variability of the weight is due to a large number of factors and can be product specific.

The team should update Phase I control charts parameter estimates periodically.

10.2.6   Interpret $\bar{x} - R$ Chart

- The mean chart (Figure 10.1) depicts that the process of the filling in this product consists of a high giveaway as most of the points plotted above the upper control limit. Commonly the food packer will decide to adjust the charts initial level (phase I monitoring).

  Action plan. Implementing Phase I of control chart: Resample to estimate the process parameters before implementing the control chart for real-time monitoring. A large number of out-of-control situation may be due to

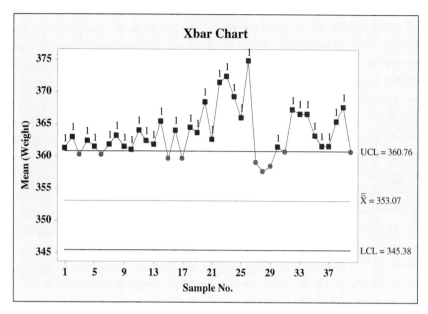

Figure 10.1 X-bar chart.

the incorrect measurements and of readjustment of the process by operators. The later factor is the reason for out-of-control situation as the target
weight is 350 g. It is common in the food industry to overfill or oversupply
the packages as an economic strategy to avoid any regulation breach.

- There is an apparent shift of variation level after sample 21, where the variation level has fluctuated a more than the previous data points. Refer to
Figure 10.2 (starting sample 21).
- *Action plan.* the non-random unusual points of variation should be investigated in the case that non-standard data has been included. Commonly, the
factors causing variation in the processes are due to the equipment capability and food quality characteristics such as the texture of the product and
presence/non-presence of discrete particulate materials in the end-product.
- At the sample number 16, there is a presence of an out-of-control value on
the range chart as it shows the process standard deviation of 11.5 g and range
of 32 g. From the Table 10.1, the lowest value in the sample is 248 g which
compares to the previous data points; it does not represent the non-standard
nor inadequate weight of the package. However, there is a very high weight of
the sample, which is 350 g indicating there are 30 g of give away in the packet.
- Another two points are high value, depicting the process data is not a purely
chance occurrence.

  Action plan. The process should be investigated especially on the nonconforming sample as fish is an expensive product for the producer. The
investigation should identify the reasoning of the non-conforming sample

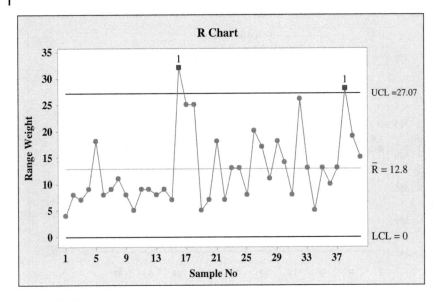

Figure 10.2 Range chart.

in order to remove the sample from the data set. Then, repeat all stages and calculations of the initial study as the sample with the out-of-control value wheel affected the subsequent calculations of target bill control.

10.2.7 Conclusion

The monitoring and control activities through the control charts are able to reduce give away, and unnecessary rejections at the checkweigher process, where the package weights are controlled before this stage. Apart from warning the employees against the violations of control limits, the other key feature of the control charts is predictive. The charts can be the tool to display trends in the subsequent sample and alert the process owner to the risk in violations, and non-random variation. As the charts are established and constructed, sample data may be taken on an on-line basis until the limits need to be recalculated.

10.3 Case Study 2 Monitoring the Sausage Production

10.3.1 Problem Statement

In order to understand and analyse the main problem of sausage production, voice of the customers have been collected and analysed through Pareto analysis to prioritise the main issues and problems. The marketing department has provided a survey on the customer complaints on the sausage.

The characteristics that are considered as defective sausages are due to the bland flavour, rancid, poor texture, broken sausage, too oily, opening of bag, pinholes, and air pockets.

10.3.2 Processes

The sausage is processed and prepared from meat, fat, and spices and it was prepared following a specific recipe. It is imperative for the process owners and businesses to fully understand the steps and details involved in their processes. In this case, the company is reluctant to assign a technical expert in drawing the flowchart; instead inviting all the people involved and who perform the process on a daily basis. The flowchart identified the steps involve in sausage processing; mincing, resting, kneading, filling, ripening, storage, and transportation as depicted in the Figure 10.3.

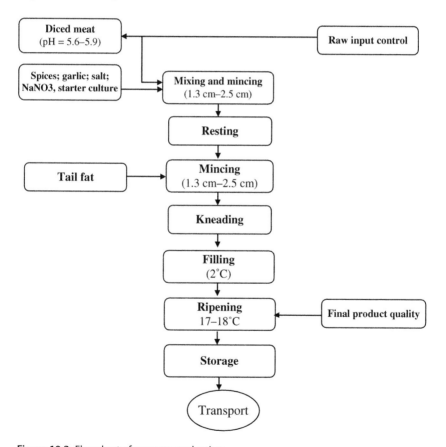

Figure 10.3 Flowchart of sausage production.

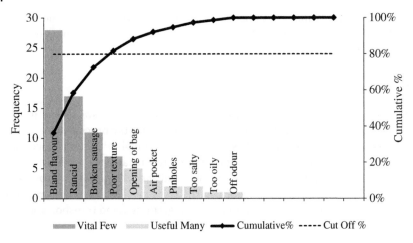

Figure 10.4 Pareto analysis of consumer complaints.

The steps involved in the sausage processing are screened through to identify the key process to be monitored. Flowchart or process mapping is a convenient approach to identify the key processes involved in the production of the products. In this case, quality control points are at material input and final product control. One of the important points before the product arrived at the consumers, final product quality control is a critical point that may assess all critical quality characteristics prioritised in the Pareto analysis (Figure 10.4).

10.3.3 Sampling

Sausages were inspected at each shift for 15 shifts. The inspector recorded the number of defective sausages in each shift. Note that the number of sausages inspected varies in each shift.

Sample sizes for p-chart should be large >50, to be able to detect moderate shift of mean.

10.3.4 Type of Data

In the food industry there are quality characteristics that are non-measurable type which accordingly will be classified into two categories, which are in this case the defective and non-defective sausages. As identified in the problem statement (Section 10.3.1), the critical quality characteristics based on the Pareto analysis, are not measurable. The data recorded in the process is the percentage of non-conforming items after inspecting the sausages. The management is interested to understand the trend of the sausage production

Table 10.2 Data defectives sausages from the inspection.

Shift	Inspected	No of defectives	Fraction, p	Shift	Inspected	No of defectives	Fraction, p
1	210	40	0.190476				
2	220	28	0.127273	9	230	16	0.0695652
3	272	15	0.055147	10	271	17	0.0627306
4	120	23	0.191667	11	308	19	0.0616883
5	149	20	0.134228	12	258	20	0.0775194
6	208	21	0.100962	13	301	16	0.0531561
7	310	19	0.061290	14	250	14	0.0560000
8	172	15	0.087209	15	268	15	0.0559701

- The first column is the shift number.
- The second column is the number of sausage inspected.
- The third column is the number of defect sausages.
- The fourth column is the fraction of the defective sausages.

quality, which suggests the appropriateness of control chart application. In this case, defective fraction refers to the ratio of the number of defective inspection series to the total number of products that are inspected. Table 10.1 displays the sample size, number of defective sausage and the calculated defective fraction (Table 10.2).

10.3.5 Construct Control Chart

In order to assess the quality of the sausage products in fraction defectives in each inspected shift, a p-chart is constructed. The chart is applied in the situation where a variety of product samples are inspected, also the frequency of sampling in hourly, shifts or days. P-chart is applied to have a clear idea of view of the products' quality history base on the fraction defectives that are expressed in percentages.

p-chart formula:

$$\bar{p} = \frac{Total\ number\ of\ defective\ units\ in\ the\ samples}{Total\ number\ of\ the\ sample\ units}$$

$$Control\ limits = \bar{p} \pm 3 \left(\sqrt{\frac{\bar{p}(1-\bar{p})}{n}} \right)$$

Control limits portrayed the upper and control limits. The values of p determined in the experiments between these limits with approximately 99.7% probability.

Before developing the control chart, type of control chart was chosen based on the type of data and number of samples. The *p*-chart is constructed based on the normal curve approximation of binomial distribution model.

In this case, as the sample size varies, the UCL and LCL are not straight lines, but appear in step shapes. This is one of the important considerations of using the chart as the plotting is in the percentage of defective regardless of the size of the sample in each subgroup.

10.3.6   Interpreting the *p*-Chart

Figure 10.5 shows the *p-chart* sausages with $\bar{p} = 0.0840$, or 6.39% the centerline where the fraction defectives vary. The lower control limit and upper control limit are populated and showed for each shift. The data points are the fraction defectives for each shift in order to assess the process control of sausages production. The figure also shows that there are two points outside of the control limits at the first and fourth shift using the rules and the point that is exceeding 3σ upper and lower limit. The fraction defectives reside well within the control limits for the remaining shifts. However, the charts show after the eighth shift, the fraction defectives are plotted less then centerline, which calls for readjustment of the machine. At this point, the investigation of the assignable cause should be implemented; corrective action should be taken following the out-of-control-action-plan. Later, it is necessary to calculate modified control limits for the next set of shifts, provided the out-of-control situation is due to the assignable cause. The modified control charts are constructed using the new

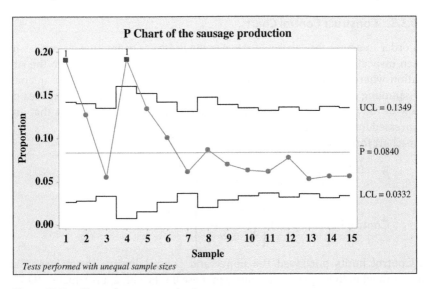

Figure 10.5 p-Chart of sausage production.

$\bar{p} = 0.0691$. On the other hand, if the value of p is known or targeted in advance, this value of p is used directly to calculate the control limits instead of letting the software estimate the mean value. The feedback action should be taken where investigations at the out-of-control-point is critical. It was identified that new contract workers are assigned at the shift number 1–2 and number 4–5, which explained high number of defects. The out-of-control point due to this reason also affects the process performance at shift number 2 and shift the number 5 where both points are closed to the upper control limit.

Activating all alarm signs increases the risk of false alarm.

10.3.7 Conclusion

• The processes for the sausage production are not statically stable as the proportion of defective sausages was identified exceeding the control limit.
• The quality criteria for sausage production is unmeasurable which therefore the inspection is based on two categories, which are defective and non-defective products (attribute data).
• Along the monitoring and control of the processes, several other quality techniques are applied to improve the process and achieve stability of the process (e.g. flowchart, Pareto analysis, cause and effect analysis).
• The advantage of using p-chart in this case is multiple key quality characteristics can be integrated in one chart.

10.4 Case Study 3 Controlling Microbiological Hazards on the Food Products

10.4.1 Problem Statement

• Hazard Analysis Critical Control Point (HACCP) is an approach used by many for the food safety purposes. A rapid hygiene testing system through adenosine triphosphate (ATP) Bioluminescence is implemented to monitor and control the hygiene level of selected control points in the HACCP system real-time data. Relative Light Units (RLUs) is the type of data that provide the amount of microbial to determine the hygienic status through comparison of the maximum RLU value (determined previous evolution tests) on the Pass/Fail basis. In the conventional practice, such a system is able to prevent the failed control point from the operation. However, the system unable to provide warning when there is a potential for out-of-control situation in cleaning the plant. Out-of-control situation is interpreted as the microbial amount is too high, and then the plan view to be not properly cleaned.

- In order to establish a statistical trend analysis instead of just Pass/Fail information, SPC charts should be employed. Based on the conventional SPC charts, the charts are unable to analyse the RLU data, as the size of the data is equal to 1 (single measurement) and the data is not following normal distribution. However, the data can provide useful information through the usage of alternative charts that supports single measurement data (e.g. individual chart, CUSUM).

10.4.2 Process

The process highlight is captured in the dairy farm. The CP identified is the milk-filling machine and the process that is highly related to the food safety is cleaning the machines.

10.4.3 Sampling

- The RLU data was collected approximately for three months and the data were analysed to construct trend analysis for the process.
- Sample size, $n = 1$

10.4.4 Type of Data

- The data collected is a continuous data based on the value of RLU.
- The assumption to the usage of the chart is, the data is following normal distribution, and it is even essential for the single measurement data. However, for exploratory analysis, normality assumption may not be applicable, where in this case, the interpreting of the raw data should be done with caution.
- Action can be taken by transforming the original data to that following normal distribution more closely.
- There are several options for the transformation from the Poisson distribution is by taking square roots of the data. The transformation is in order to reduce the overall noise in the observation.

10.4.5 Construct Control Chart

In order to construct a control chart, in order to choose the appropriate type of control chart, the type of the data needs to be identified (refer Figure 9.5).

10.4.5.1 Modification of the Data

There are options in modifying the data, which can be done through logarithmic transformation and square root the raw data (refer to Appendix A).

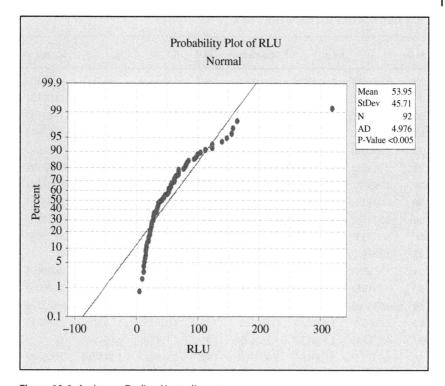

Figure 10.6 Anderson-Darling Normality test.

Figure 10.6 shows that the raw data does not follow normal distribution as through the Anderson-Darling test, p-val <0.005. The deduction is based on the hypothesis:

- Hypothesis *null*. The data is following normal distribution.
- Hypothesis *alternative*. The data is not following normal distribution

Since the p-val is less than 0.05 at 5% level of significance, the hypothesis null is rejected, which concludes the data is not following normal distribution. Modification of the data is required to transform the data following normal distribution. The modification is implemented using several types of transformation compared in the Tables 10.3 and 10.4.

Based on the comparison of the raw data and transformed data, the normality test through Anderson-Darling shows that both the raw RLU data and the transformed square root data do not follow normal distribution. The control chart is then developed based on the logarithmic transformation data. Individual chart and CUSUM plot and CUSUM control chart of the transformed data are displayed in Figures 10.7–10.9.

Table 10.3 Raw data and transformed data.

RLU	ln	Lg	Square root	RLU	ln	lg	Square root
23	3.135494	1.361728	4.795832	147	4.990433	2.167317	12.12436
46	3.828641	1.662758	6.78233	13	2.564949	1.113943	3.605551
39	3.663562	1.591065	6.244998	12	2.484907	1.079181	3.464102
62	4.127134	1.792392	7.874008	15	2.70805	1.176091	3.872983
33	3.496508	1.518514	5.744563	14	2.639057	1.146128	3.741657
21	3.044522	1.322219	4.582576	76	4.330733	1.880814	8.717798
20	2.995732	1.30103	4.472136	28	3.332205	1.447158	5.291503
56	4.025352	1.748188	7.483315	29	3.367296	1.462398	5.385165
69	4.234107	1.838849	8.306624	44	3.78419	1.643453	6.63325
26	3.258097	1.414973	5.09902	15	2.70805	1.176091	3.872983
27	3.295837	1.431364	5.196152	16	2.772589	1.20412	4
24	3.178054	1.380211	4.898979	123	4.812184	2.089905	11.09054
22	3.091042	1.342423	4.690416	5	1.609438	0.69897	2.236068
69	4.234107	1.838849	8.306624	41	3.713572	1.612784	6.403124
42	3.73767	1.623249	6.480741	56	4.025352	1.748188	7.483315
97	4.574711	1.986772	9.848858	9	2.197225	0.954243	3
56	4.025352	1.748188	7.483315	82	4.406719	1.913814	9.055385
33	3.496508	1.518514	5.744563	22	3.091042	1.342423	4.690416
33	3.496508	1.518514	5.744563	22	3.091042	1.342423	4.690416
69	4.234107	1.838849	8.306624	63	4.143135	1.799341	7.937254
24	3.178054	1.380211	4.898979	85	4.442651	1.929419	9.219544
34	3.526361	1.531479	5.830952	34	3.526361	1.531479	5.830952
29	3.367296	1.462398	5.385165	158	5.062595	2.198657	12.56981
29	3.367296	1.462398	5.385165	164	5.099866	2.214844	12.80625
19	2.944439	1.278754	4.358899	155	5.043425	2.190332	12.4499
57	4.043051	1.755875	7.549834	79	4.369448	1.897627	8.888194
81	4.394449	1.908485	9	94	4.543295	1.973128	9.69536
99	4.59512	1.995635	9.949874	319	5.765191	2.503791	17.86057
43	3.7612	1.633468	6.557439	38	3.637586	1.579784	6.164414
80	4.382027	1.90309	8.944272	19	2.944439	1.278754	4.358899
68	4.219508	1.832509	8.246211	64	4.158883	1.80618	8
112	4.718499	2.049218	10.58301	50	3.912023	1.69897	7.071068
25	3.218876	1.39794	5	16	2.772589	1.20412	4
52	3.951244	1.716003	7.211103	25	3.218876	1.39794	5
24	3.178054	1.380211	4.898979	28	3.332205	1.447158	5.291503
35	3.555348	1.544068	5.91608	35	3.555348	1.544068	5.91608

(Continued)

Table 10.3 (Continued)

RLU	ln	Lg	Square root	RLU	ln	lg	Square root
15	2.70805	1.176091	3.872983	52	3.951244	1.716003	7.211103
47	3.850148	1.672098	6.855655	28	3.332205	1.447158	5.291503
104	4.644391	2.017033	10.19804	35	3.555348	1.544068	5.91608
53	3.970292	1.724276	7.28011	52	3.951244	1.716003	7.211103
51	3.931826	1.70757	7.141428	139	4.934474	2.143015	11.78983
34	3.526361	1.531479	5.830952	59	4.077537	1.770852	7.681146
17	2.833213	1.230449	4.123106	62	4.127134	1.792392	7.874008
62	4.127134	1.792392	7.874008	55	4.007333	1.740363	7.416198
23	3.135494	1.361728	4.795832	12	2.484907	1.079181	3.464102
123	4.812184	2.089905	11.09054	147	4.990433	2.167317	12.12436

Normality test for each of the transformed data in Table 10.4. (Refer to Appendix B).

Table 10.4 The data distribution for net weight fish packaging.

	RLU	Ln	Lg	Square root
Normality test	<0.005	0.901	0.901	<0.005
Standard deviation	45.71	0.7404	0.3216	2.63

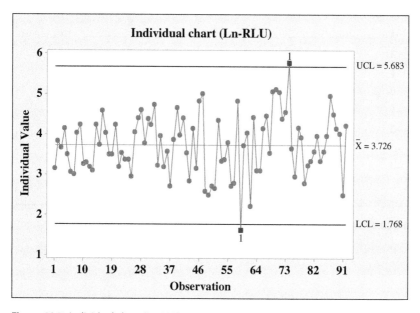

Figure 10.7 Individual chart (Ln-RLU).

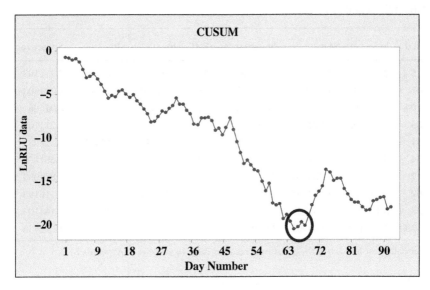

Figure 10.8 CUSUM plot of the ATP data (Ln-RLU).

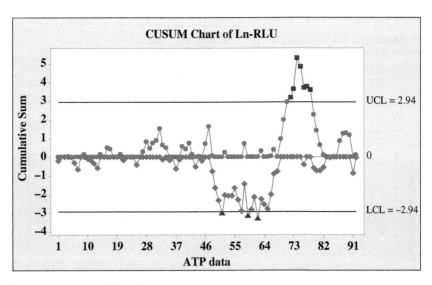

Figure 10.9 CUSUM chart of the ATP data.

10.4.6   Interpret the Charts

10.4.6.1   The Individuals Chart

Interpreting the trend may prevent any out-of-control event. Point of the day 65 onward indicate the development of a potential problem, before it occurred.

Considering the appropriateness of the monitoring scheme, a Shewhart control charts for individuals is a good option due to its simplicity. However, there are more sophisticated control charts such as CUSUM and exponentially weighted moving average (EWMA) that are sensitive in detecting small changes (Montgomery, 2012). Based on the Figure 10.5, the chart shows the poor consistency of the readings where there are values which exceed the limit of the arbitrary control limit value of the RLU, set preceding to the routine use of the system on Day 60 and Day 74. The control chart shows that the individual values exceed the limit but fails to indicate any significant adverse trends. To develop the chart in the Minitab please refer to Appendix C.

10.4.6.2   The CUSUM Control Chart

The chart shows trend of the process, where it is easier to predict and indicate if the process is going to be out-of-control before it could happen. The plots in Figure 10.8 show there is a mean shift (points in red circle) which indicates a potential out-of-control process. However, such plots are unable to clearly indicate the limits that will indicate the process potential for an out-of-control condition.

For Figure 10.9, the process is in control when the values are close to zero. If the points in the chart move up and down, where the values will occur more positive or negative will lead to the detection of special causes. Compared to other types of charts, in the case of SPC, if there is a tendency of the points to be above and below the centerline (zero line), there is a potential that the process average has shifted and therefore, the process owner must investigate the cause contributed to such a situation. Such situations may occur due to errors in registering the data, instruments and machines are not calibrated equipment operator error or error in the data collection technique.

Any point that exceeded the control limits indicate an out-of-control situation. The CUSUM chart in Figure 10.8, indicate out-of-control from at the point 51, 54, and 59 for the lower control limit and from the point 72 to point 78 (upper control limit).

One of the alternative procedures of CUSUM is through the V-mask control scheme proposed by Bernard in 1959. The chart contains plotted points (cumulative sum of deviations of the raw data from the target) and V-mask (apply state of control limits in determining the art of control points). However, according to (Montgomery, 2012). V-mask procedure for CUSUM is not strongly advised to be applied due to its disadvantages:

- A practical approach by the industry, headstart feature is unable to be applied through the usage of V-mask.
- It is difficult to determine how far the arm of the V-mask should extend.
- It is ambiguous to assign the α and β value.

One of the critical disadvantages of CUSUM is the underlying raw data are lost. This is due the mechanism behind the construction of CUSUM control charts based on the sum of the deviations of the points from the target value that limits its ability to portray the underlying process behaviour.

Based on the control charts above, there is a clear advance warning that Day 72 will be out-of-control. By using the control charts, fail situation as such Day 72 onwards may be prevented if preventive action is applied on previous days (e.g. increasing trend).

10.4.7 Conclusion

This case study suggests the potential of integrating SPC with HACCP system in monitoring and controlling food safety, further enhance preventive practice that is preached in continuous improvement philosophy through a systematic trend analysis and the usage of data-based approach (control chart) as the decision- making tool. This case study also demystifies the inappropriateness of the application of control charts with the food industry data.

References

Abdolvand, N., Albadvi, A., and Ferdowsi, Z. (2008). Assessing readiness for business process reengineering. *Business Process Management Journal* 14 (4): 497–511.

Abdul Halim Lim, S., Antony, J., He, Z., and Arshed, N. (2017). Critical observations on the statistical process control implementation in the UK food industry: a survey. *International Journal of Quality and Reliability Management* 34 (5): 684–700.

Ahire, S.L. and Ravichandran, T. (2001). An innovation diffusion model of TQM implementation. *IEEE Transactions on Engineering Management* 48 (4): 445–464.

Anderson, J.C., Rungtusanatham, M., and Schroeder, R.G. (1994). A theory of quality management underlying the Deming management method. *Academy of Management Review* 19 (3): 472–509.

Antony, J. (2000). Ten key ingredients for making SPC successful in organisations. *Measuring Business Excellence* 4: 7–10.

Antony, J. (2014). Readiness factors for the Lean Six Sigma journey in the higher education sector. *International Journal of Productivity and Performance Management* 63 (2): 257–264.

Antony, J. and Balbontin, A. (2000). Key ingredients for the effective implementation of statistical process control. *Work Study* 49 (6): 242–247.

Antony, J. and Taner, T. (2003). A conceptual framework for the effective implementation of statistical process control. *Business Process Management Journal* 9 (4): 473–489.

Appelbaum, S.H., Habashy, S., Malo, J.-L., and Shafiq, H. (2012). Back to the future: revisiting Kotter's 1996 change model. *Journal of Management Development* 31 (8): 764–782.

Argote, L. and Miron-Spektor, E. (2011). Organizational learning: from experience to knowledge. *Organization Science* 22 (5): 1123–1137.

Argyris, C. (1995). Action science and organizational learning. *Journal of Managerial Psychology* 10 (6): 20–26.

Statistical Process Control for the Food Industry: A Guide for Practitioners and Managers, First Edition.
Sarina Abdul Halim Lim and Jiju Antony.
© 2019 John Wiley & Sons Ltd. Published 2019 by John Wiley & Sons Ltd.

Argyris, C. and Schön, D.A. (1978). *Organizational Learning: A Theory of Action Perspective*, vol. 173. Reading, MA: Addison-Wesley.

Armenakis, A.A., Harris, S.G., and Mossholder, K.W. (1993). Creating readiness for organizational change. *Human Relations* 46 (6): 681–703.

Baird-Parker, A.C. and Mayes, T. (1989). Application of HACCP to assure microbiological safety. *Food Science and Technology Today* 3: 23–26.

Bandura, A. (1993). Perceived self-efficacy in cognitive development and functioning. *Educational Psychologist* 28 (2): 117–148.

Barker, R. (1990). SPC and total quality management. *Total Quality Management* 1 (2): 37–41.

Barone, S. and Franco, E.L. (2012). *Statistical and Managerial Techniques for Six Sigma Methodology: Theory and Application*. Wiley.

Bernard, D. and Scott, V.N. (2007). Hazard analysis and critical control point system: use in controlling microbiological hazards. In: *Food Microbiology: Fundamentals and Frontiers*, 3e (ed. M.P. Doyle and L.R. Beuchat), 971–985. American Society of Microbiology.

Bessant, J. and Francis, D. (1999). Developing strategic continuous improvement capability. *International Journal of Operations and Production Management* 19 (11): 1106–1119.

Bidder, P.L. (1990). Experiences of introducing SPC in a confectionery factory. In: *Applied statistical process control, IEE colloquium on*, 1–2. London: IEEEXplore.

Bissell, D. (1994). *Statistical Methods for SPC and TQM*, vol. 26. CRC Press.

Bjerke, F.R. and Hersleth, M. (2001). Introducing statistical thinking to the food industry–facilitating and inhibiting factors. *Quality management journal* 8 (3): 49–60.

Blackman, D., Connelly, J., and Henderson, S. (2004). Does double loop learning create reliable knowledge? *The Learning Organization* 11 (1): 11–27.

Bourlakis, M.A. and Weightman, P.W. (2008). *Food Supply Chain Management*. Wiley.

Brannstrom-Stenberg, A. and Deleryd, M (1999). Implementation of statistical process control and process capability studies: requirements or free will? *Total Quality Management and Business Excellent* 10 (4–5): 439–446.

Buckler, B. (1996). A learning process model to achieve continuous improvement and innovation. *The Learning Organization* 3 (3): 31–39.

Bushe, G.R. (1988). Cultural contradictions of statistical process control in American manufacturing organizations. *Journal of Management* 14 (1): 19–31.

Castagliola, P. and Vännman, K. (2007). Monitoring capability indices using an EWMA approach. *Quality and Reliability Engineering International* 23 (7): 769–790.

Caswell, J.A., Bredahl, M.E., and Hooker, N.H. (1998). How quality management metasystems are affecting the food industry. *Review of Agricultural Economics* 20: 547.

Cheng, P.C.-H. and Dawson, S.D. (1998). A study of statistical process control: practice, problems and training needs. *Total Quality Management* 9 (1): 3–20.

Choo, A.S., Linderman, K.W., and Schroeder, R.G. (2007). Method and context perspectives on learning and knowledge creation in quality management. *Journal of Operations Management* 25 (4): 918–931.

Clarke, R. (1999). *A Primer in Diffusion of Innovations Theory*. Xamax Consultancy Pty Ltd.

Clute, M. (2008). *Food industry quality control systems*. Boca Raton: CRC press.

Coch, L. and French, J.R. Jr. (1948). Overcoming resistance to change. *Human Relations* 1 (4): 512–532.

Cohen, S.G. and Bailey, D.E. (1997). What makes teams work: group effectiveness research from the shop floor to the executive suite. *Journal of Management* 23 (3): 239–290.

Cox, D. and Efron, B. (2017). Statistical thinking for 21st century scientists. *Science Advances* 3 (6): e1700768.

Crosby Philip, B. (1984). *Quality without tears: The art of hassle-free management*. New York: McGraw-Hill.

Dale, B.G. and Lascelles, D.M. (1997). Total quality management adoption: revisiting the levels. *The TQM Magazine* 9 (6): 418–428.

Dale, B. and Shaw, P. (1989). The application of statistical process control in UK automotive manufacture: some research findings. *Quality and Reliability Engineering International* 5 (1): 5–15.

Dale, B.G. and Shaw, P. (1992). Statistical process control in PCB manufacture: what are the lessons? *IEE Proceedings A Science, Measurement and Technology* 139: 182.

Dale, B.G. and Smith, M. (1997). Spectrum of quality management implementation grid: development and use. *Managing Service Quality: An International Journal* 7 (6): 307–311.

Dalgiç, A.C., Vardin, H., and BelibaÄŸli, K. (2011). Improvement of food safety and quality by statistical process control (SPC) in food processing systems: a case study of traditional Sucuk (Sausage). In: *Processing, Quality Control of Herbal Medicines and Related Areas* (ed. Y. Shoyama), 978–953. Retrieved from https://www.intechopen.com/books/quality-control-of-herbal-medicines-and-related-areas.

Dalton, C.C. and Gottlieb, L.N. (2003). The concept of readiness to change. *Journal of Advanced Nursing* 42 (2): 108–117.

Daniel, R.H. (1961). Management data crisis. *Harvard Business Review*, September-October:111–112.

Davis, J. and Ryan, M. (2005). Training in the SME sector of the food and drink manufacturing industries. *Management Services*, 4, 38–42.

Deloitte Touche Tohmatsu Ltd (2013). *The food value chain: A challenge for the next century*. London: The Creative Studio.

Deming, W. (1986). *Out of the Crisis*. Cambridge, MA: itd: Massachusetts Institute of Technology Press: MIT Press.

Denton, J. (1998). *Organisational Learning and Effectiveness*. Psychology Press.

van der Spiegel, M., Luning, P.A., Ziggers, G.W., and Jongen, W.M.F. (2003). Towards a conceptual model to measure effectiveness of food quality systems. *Trends in Food Science and Technology* 14 (10): 424–431.

Does, R. and Trip, A. (1997). A framework for implementation of statistical process control. *International Journal of Quality Science* 2 (4): 181–198.

Does, R.J., Roes, C.B., and Trip, A. (1999). *Statistical Process Control in Industry: Implementation and Assurance of SPC*, vol. 5. Springer Science and Business.

Dogdu, S., Santos, D.L., and Dougherty, T. (1997). *Guidelines for implementing statistical process control in printed circuit board manufacturing*. Paper presented at the 1997 International Symposium on Mocroelectronics.

Dora, M., Kumar, M., Van Goubergen, D. et al. (2013a). Food quality management system: reviewing assessment strategies and a feasibility study for European food small and medium-sized enterprises. *Food Control* 31 (2): 607–616.

Dora, M., Kumar, M., Van Goubergen, D. et al. (2013b). Operational performance and critical success factors of lean manufacturing in European food processing SMEs. *Trends in Food Science and Technology* 31 (2): 156–164.

Early, R. (2012). *Guide to Quality Management Systems for the Food Industry*. Springer Science and Business Media.

Edith, I.N. and Ochubiojo, E.M. (2012). Food quality control: history, present and future. In: *Scientific, Health and Social Aspects of the Food Industry* (ed. B. Valdez), 421–429. InTech.

Efstratiadis, M., Karirti, A.C., Arvanitoyannis, I.S., and Michalis (2000). Implementation of ISO 9000 to the food industry: an overview. *International Journal of Food Sciences and Nutrition* 51 (6): 459–473.

Ehigie, B.O. and McAndrew, E.B. (2005). Innovation, diffusion and adoption of total quality management (TQM). *Management Decision* 43 (6): 925–940.

Elg, M., Olsson, J., and Dahlgaard, J.J. (2008). Implementing statistical process control: an organizational perspective. *International Journal of Quality and Reliability Management* 25 (6): 545–560.

Elrod, P.D. and Tippett, D.D. (1999). An empirical study of the relationship between team performance and team maturity. *Engineering Management Journal* 11 (1): 7–14.

Ewan, W.D. (1963). When and how to use cu-sum charts. *Technometrics*, 5(1), 1–22.

Fine, C.H. (1986). Quality improvement and learning in productive systems. *Management Science* 32 (10): 1301–1315.

Fine, C.H. (1988). A quality control model with learning effects. *Operations Research* 36 (3): 437–444.

Fortune, A.E., Reid, W.J., and Miller, R. (2013). *Qualitative Research in Social Work*. Columbia University Press.

Frigon, N.L. and Mathews, D. (1997). *Practical guide to experimental design*. Wiley.

Gan, F.F. (1991a). An optimal design of CUSUM quality control charts. *Journal of Quality Technology* 23 (4): 279–286.

Gaspar, P.D., Pinheiro, R., Domingues, C. et al. (2015). Training requirements for agro-food industry in Portugal. *International Journal of Food Studies* 4 (1).

Gijo, E. (2005). Improving process capability of manufacturing process by application of statistical techniques. *Quality Engineering* 17 (2): 309–315.

Grigg, N.P. (1998). Statistical process control in UK food production: an overview. *International Journal of Quality and Reliability Management* 15 (2): 223–238.

Grigg, N.P. and Walls, L. (2007a). Developing statistical thinking for performance improvement in the food industry. *International Journal of Quality and Reliability Management* 24 (4): 347–369.

Grigg, N.P. and Walls, L. (2007b). The role of control charts in promoting organisational learning: new perspectives from a food industry study. *The TQM Magazine* 19 (1): 37–49.

Grigg, N.P., Daly, J., and Stewart, M. (1998). Case study: the use of statistical process control in fish product packaging. *Food control* 9 (5): 289–298.

Grunert, K.G. (2005). Food quality and safety: consumer perception and demand. *European Review of Agricultural Economics* 32 (3): 369–391.

Grunert, K.G., Larsen, H.H., Madsen, T.K., and Baadsgaard, A. (1995). *Market Orientation in Food and Agriculture*. Springer Science and Business Media.

Gurumurthy, A., Mazumdar, P., and Muthusubramanian, S. (2013). Graph theoretic approach for analysing the readiness of an organisation for adapting lean thinking: a case study. *International Journal of Organizational Analysis* 21 (3): 396–427.

Hackman, J.R. (1987). The design of work teams. In: *Handbook of Organizational Behavior* (ed. J. Lorsch). Englewood Cliffs, NJ: Prentice-Hall.

Halim Lim, S.A., Antony, J., Arshed, N., and Albliwi, S. (2017). A systematic review of statistical process control implementation in the food manufacturing industry. *Total Quality Management and Business Excellence* 28 (1–2): 176–189.

Harcourt, A. and Brace, D. (2011). *The American Heritage Dictionary of the English Language*. Boston: Houghton Mifflin.

Harris, C. (1994). Successfully implementing statistical process control in integrated steel companies. *Interfaces* 24: 49–58.

Hawkins, D.M. (1981). A CUSUM for a scale parameter. *Journal of Quality Technology* 13 (4): 228–231.

Hawkins, D.M. (1993). Cumulative sum control charting: an underutilized SPC tool. *Quality Engineering* 5 (3): 463–477.

Hayes, G., Scallan, A., and Wong, J. (1997). Applying statistical process control to monitor and evaluate the hazard analysis critical control point hygiene data. *Food Control* 8 (4): 173–176.

Herschdoerfer, S. (1967). *Quality Control in the Food Industry*, vol. 1. London: Academic Press.

Herscovitch, L. and Meyer, J.P. (2002). Commitment to organizational change: extension of a three-component model. *Journal of Applied Psychology* 87 (3): 474.

Hewson, C., O'Sullivan, P., and Stenning, K. (1996). Training needs associated with statistical process control. *Training for Quality* 4 (4): 32–36.

Hoerl, R. (1995). Enhancing the bottom-line impact of statistical methods. *Quality Management Journal* 2 (4): 58–74.

Holt, D.T., Armenakis, A.A., Feild, H.S., and Harris, S.G. (2007). Readiness for organizational change the systematic development of a scale. *The Journal of Applied Behavioral Science* 43 (2): 232–255.

Holt, D.T., Armenakis, A.A., Harris, S.G., and Feild, H.S. (2007). Toward a comprehensive definition of readiness for change: a review of research and instrumentation. *Research in Organizational Change and Development* 14: 289–336.

Hood, W.W. and Wilson, C.S. (2001). The literature of bibliometrics, scientometrics, and informetrics. *Scientometrics* 52 (2): 291–314.

Hryniewicz, O. (1997). Statistical process control with the help of international statistical standards. *Human System Management* 16: 201.

Hubbard, M.R. (1999). *Statistical quality control for the food industry*. New York: Kluwer Academic/Plenum Publishers.

Hubbard, M.R. (2003). *Statistical Quality Control for Food Industry*, 3e. New York: Kluwer Academic/Plenum Publishers.

Hubbard, M.R. (2013). *Statistical Quality Control for Food Industry*. Aspen Publishers.

Hung, H.-C. and Sung, M.-H. (2011). Applying six sigma to manufacturing processes in the food industry to reduce quality cost. *Scientific Research and Essays* 6: 580–591.

Hurst, W. and Harris, L. (2013). Integrating hazard analysis critical control point (HACCP) and statistical process control (SPC) for safer nut processing. In: *Improving the Safety and Quality of Nuts, Improving the Safety and Quality of Nuts* (ed. L.J. Harris), 119–147. Woodhead Publishing Limited.

Hutchins, R. (1997). Category management in the food industry: a research agenda. *British Food Journal* 99: 177–180.

Ittner, C.D. and Larcker, D.F. (1997). The performance effects of process management techniques. *Management Science* 43 (4): 522–553.

Jacobson, E.H. (1957). *The effect of changing industrial methods and automation on personnel*. Paper presented at the Symposium on Preventive and Social Psychology, Washington, DC.

Jeliazkova, M. and Westerheijden, D.F. (2002). Systemic adaptation to a changing environment: towards a next generation of quality assurance models. *Higher Education* 44 (3–4): 433–448.

Kappelman, L.A., Prybutok, V.R., and von Dran, G.M. (1993). Empowerment and successful management of an organizational change: the case of a bank acquisition. *Management Research News* 19 (7): 23–36.

Kaye, M.M. and Dyason, M.D. (1995). The fifth era. *The TQM Magazine* 7 (1): 33–37.

Kennedy, G., Nantel, G., and Shetty, P. (2004). Globalization of Food Systems in Developing Countries: Impact on Food Security and Nutrition. Food and Agriculture Organization.

Kerber, K. and Buono, A.F. (2005). Rethinking organizational change: reframing the challenge of change management. *Organization Development Journal* 23 (3): 23.

Kerlinger, F.N. (1986). *Foundations of Behavioral Research*. Fort Worth, TX: Holt, Rinehart and Winston: Inc.

Kirkpatrick, D.L. (1979). Techniques for evaluating training programs. *Training and Development Journal* 33 (6): 78–92.

Knowles, G., Johnson, M., and Warwood, S. (2004). Medicated sweet variability: a six sigma application at a UK food manufacturer. *The TQM Magazine* 16: 284–292.

Kolesar, P. (1993). The relevance of research on statistical process control to the total quality movement. *Journal of Engineering and Technology Management* 10: 317–338.

Kontoghiorghes, C. (2001). Factors affecting training effectiveness in the context of the introduction of new technology—a US case study. *International Journal of Training and Development* 5 (4): 248–260.

Kotter, J.P. (1996). *Leading Change*. Harvard Business Press.

Kotter, J.P. (2008a). *Force for Change: How Leadership Differs from Management*. New York: Simon and Schuster Inc.

Kotter, J.P. (2008b). *A Sense of Urgency*. Harvard Business Press.

Kotter, J.P. and Schlesinger, L.A. (2008). Choosing strategies for change. *Harvard Business Review* 86 (7/8): 130.

Kovach, T. and Cho, R. (2011). Better processes make good eats the food industry can benefit from lean Six Sigma principles. *Industrial Engineer* 43 (1): 36.

Krüger, V. (1999). Towards a European definition of TQM—a historical review. *The TQM Magazine* 11: 257–263.

Krumwiede, D. and Sheu, C. (1996). Implementing SPC in a small organization: a TQM approach. *Integrated Manufacturing Systems* 7: 45–51.

Kumar, S. and Gupta, Y. (1993). Statistical process control at Motorola's Austin assembly plant. *Interfaces* 23: 84–92.

Kumar, A. and Motwani, J. (1996). Doing it right the second time. *Industrial Management and Data Systems* 96: 14–19.

Lagrosen, Y., Chebl, R., and Tuesta, M.R. (2011). Organisational learning and Six Sigma deployment readiness evaluation: a case study. *International Journal of Lean Six Sigma* 2 (1): 23–40.

Lamikanra, O. (2002). *Fresh-Cut Fruits and Vegetables: Science, Technology, and Market*. Florida: CRC Press.

Lee, H.-H. and Lee, C.-Y. (2014). The effects of total quality management and organisational learning on business performance: evidence from Taiwanese insurance industries. *Total Quality Management and Business Excellence* 25 (9–10): 1072–1087.

Lee, G., Bennett, D., and Oakes, I. (2000). Technological and organisational change in small-to medium-sized manufacturing companies: a learning organisation perspective. *International Journal of Operations and Production Management* 20 (5): 549–572.

Lewin, K. (1947). Frontiers in group dynamics. *Human Relations* 1: 5–41.

Lim, S.A.H. and Antony, J. (2016). Statistical process control readiness in the food industry: development of a self-assessment tool. *Trends in Food Science and Technology* 58: 133–139.

Lim, S.A.H., Antony, J., and Albliwi, S. (2014). Statistical process control (SPC) in the food industry–a systematic review and future research agenda. *Trends in Food Science and Technology* 37 (2): 137–151.

Lim, S.A.H., Antony, J., Garza-Reyes, J.A., and Arshed, N. (2015). Towards a conceptual roadmap for statistical process control implementation in the food industry. *Trends in Food Science and Technology* 44 (1): 117–129.

Lim, S.A.H., Antony, J., and Arshed, N. (2016). A critical assessment on SPC implementation in the UK food industry. *Journal of Systemics* 14 (1): 37–42.

Locke, E.A. and Jain, V.K. (1995). Organizational learning and continuous improvement. *The International Journal of Organizational Analysis* 3 (1): 45–68.

Lucas, J.M. (1976). The design and use of V-mask control schemes. *Journal of Quality Technology* 8 (1): 1–12.

Lucey, J. (2006). Management should serve as role models for good work habits and acceptable hygienic practices. *Food Quality & Safety Magazine*. Retrieved from Food Quality & Safety Magazine website: http://www.foodquality.com

Luning, P.A. and Marcelis, W.J. (2006). A techno-managerial approach in food quality management research. *Trends in Food Science and Technology* 17 (7): 378–385.

Luning, P.A. and Marcelis, W.J. (2009). A food quality management research methodology integrating technological and managerial theories. *Trends in Food Science and Technology* 20 (1): 35–44.

Magjuka, R.J. and Baldwin, T.T. (1991). Team-based employee involvement programs: effects of design and administration. *Personnel Psychology* 44 (4): 793–812.

Mahalik, N.P. and Nambiar, A.N. (2010). Trends in food packaging and manufacturing systems and technology. *Trends in Food Science and Technology* 21 (3): 117–128.

Malone, S. (2017). *Food and Drink Federation: Representing the UK's biggest manufacturing sector.* Retrieved from https://www.fdf.org.uk/statsataglance .aspx

Maneesh, K. (2010). *Six Sigma Implementation in UK Manufacturing SMEs: An Exploratory Research.* Doctoral of Philosophy, University of Strathclyde, Glasgow.

Mann, R. and Adebanjo, O. (1998). Best practices in the food and drinks industry. *Benchmarking for Quality Management and Technology* 5 (3): 184–199.

Marquardt, M.J. (1996). *Building the Learning Organization.* McGraw-Hill Companies.

McNabb, D.E. and Sepic, F.T. (1995). Culture, climate, and total quality management: measuring readiness for change. *Public Productivity and Management Review* 369–385.

Meredith, B. (1997). *Management Teams: Why They Succeed or Fail.* Butterworth-Heinemann.

Mitra, A. (2012). *Fundamentals of Quality Control and Improvement.* NJ: Wiley.

Montgomery, D.C. (2012). *Introduction to Statistical Quality Control.* New York: Wiley.

Morgan, G. (2006). *Sociological Paradigms and Organizational Analysis.* Routledge.

Motorcu, A.R. and Gullu, A. (2006). Statistical process control in machining, a case study for machine tool capability and process capability. *Materials and Design* 27: 364–372.

Murray, S. (2007). *The world's biggest industry.* Retrieved from https://www.forbes .com/2007/11/11/growth-agriculture-business-forbeslife-food07-cx_sm_ 1113bigfood.html#111ba95373e9

Murray, P. and Chapman, R. (2003). From continuous improvement to organisational learning: developmental theory. *The Learning Organization* 10 (5): 272–282.

New World Encyclopedia. (2017). *Food industry.* Retrieved from http://www .newworldencyclopedia.org/entry/Food_industry

Noskievicova, D. (2010). Effective implementation of statistical process control. In: *Engineering the future.* InTech.

Oakland, J. and Tanner, S. (2007). A new framework for managing change. *The TQM Magazine* 19 (6): 572–589.

Ogland, P. (2014). *Mechanism Design for Total Quality Management: Using the Bootstrap Algorithm for Changing the Control Game.* Lulu. com.

Özdemir, M. and Özilgen, M. (1997). Comparison of the quality of hazelnuts unshelled with different sizing and cracking systems. *Journal of Agricultural Engineering Research* 67: 219–227.

Özilgen, M. (1998). Construction of quality control charts with sub-optimal size samples. *Food Control* 9 (1): 57–60.

Page, E.S. (1954). Continuous inspection schemes. *Biometrika* 41 (1/2): 100–115.

Page, E.S. (1961). Cumulative sum charts. *Technometrics* 3 (1): 1–9.

Paiva, C.L. (2013). Quality management: important aspects for the food industry. In: *Food Industry* (ed. I. Muzzalupo). Rijeka: InTech.

Paper, D.J., Rodger, J.A., and Pendharkar, P.C. (2001). A BPR case study at Honeywell. *Business Process Management Journal* 7 (2): 85–99.

Pereira, Z.L. and Aspinwall, E. (1991). Total Quality Control in the food industry. *Total Quality Management* 2 (2): 123–129.

Pereira, Z.L. and Aspinwall, E. (1993). Off-line quality control applied to food products. *Total Quality Management* 4: 37–41.

Pfitzer, M. and Krishnaswamy, R. (2007). The Role of the Food & Beverage Sector in Expanding Economic Opportunity. *CSR Initiative Report* 20: 9.

Radnor, Z. (2011). Implementing lean in health care: making the link between the approach, readiness and sustainability. *International Journal of Industrial Engineering and Management* 2 (1): 1–12.

Rai, B.K. (2008). Implementation of statistical process control in an Indian tea packaging company. *International Journal of Business Excellence* 1 (1): 160–174.

Raju, K.V.R. (2005). Quality control for processed food. In: *APO Seminar on Quality Control for Processed Food* (ed. K.V.R. Raju). China: Asian Productivity Organization.

Raper, P., Ashton, D., Felstead, A., and Storey, J. (1997). Towards the learning organisation? Explaining current trends in training practice in the UK. *International Journal of Training and Development* 1: 9–21.

Ren, Y., He, Z., and Luning, P.A. (2016). A systematic assessment of quality assurance-based food safety management system of Chinese edible oil manufacturer in view of context characteristics. *Total Quality Management and Business Excellence* 27 (7–8): 897–911.

Roberts, G.B., Watson, K., and Oliver, J.E. (1989). Technological innovation and organisational culture: an exploratory comparison of larger and smaller firms. *Journal of Organizational Change Management* 2 (3): 65–74.

Rockart, J. (1979). Chief executives define their own data needs. *Harvard Business Review* 57 (2): 81–93.

Rogers, E. (1995). *Diffusion of Innovations*, 5e. New York: Simon and Schuster, Inc.

Rungtusanatham, M., Anderson, J.C., and Dooley, K.J. (1997). Conceptualizing organizational implementation and practice of statistical process control. *Journal of Quality Management* 2 (1): 113–137.

Rusly, F.H., Corner, J.L., and Sun, P. (2012). Positioning change readiness in knowledge management research. *Journal of Knowledge Management* 16 (2): 329–355.

Savolainen, T. and Haikonen, A. (2007). Dynamics of organizational learning and continuous improvement in six sigma implementation. *The TQM Magazine* 19 (1): 6–17.

Schein, E.H. (2010). *Organizational Culture and Leadership*, vol. 2. Wiley.

Self, D.R. and Schraeder, M. (2009). Enhancing the success of organizational change: matching readiness strategies with sources of resistance. *Leadership and Organization Development Journal* 30 (2): 167–182.

Senge, P.M. (2006). *The Fifth Discipline: The Art and Practice of the Learning Organization*. Crown Business.

Senge, P.M. (2014). *The Fifth Discipline Fieldbook: Strategies and Tools for Building a Learning Organization*. Crown Business.

Senior, B. (1997). Team roles and team performance: is there 'really' a link? *Journal of Occupational and Organizational Psychology* 70 (3): 241–258.

Sharma, R. and Kharub, M. (2014). Attaining competitive positioning through SPC–an experimental investigation from SME. *Measuring Business Excellence* 18 (4): 86–103.

Shewhart, W. (1939). *Statistical Method: From the Viewpoint of Quality Control*. New York: Dover Publications.

Shewhart, W.A. and Deming, W.E. (1939). *Statistical Method from the Viewpoint of Quality Control*. Courier Corporation.

Shingo, S. (1986). *Zero quality control: Source inspection and the poka-yoke system*. Oregon: CRC Press.

Smith, I. (2005). Achieving readiness for organisational change. *Library Management* 26 (6/7): 408–412.

Snee, R.D. (1990). Statistical thinking and its contribution to total quality. *The American Statistician* 44 (2): 116–121.

Snee, R.D. and Hoerl, R.W. (2003). *Leading Six Sigma: A Step by Step Guide Based on Experience with GE and Other Six Sigma Companies*. Ft Press.

Srikaeo, K., Furst, J.E., and Ashton, J. (2005). Characterization of wheat-based biscuit cooking process by statistical process control techniques. *Food Control* 16 (4): 8.

Stamatis, D. (2002). *Six Sigma and Beyond the Implementation Process*, vol. VII. Edinburgh: CRC Press.

Stuart, M., Mullins, E., and Drew, E. (1996). Statistical quality control and improvement. *European Journal of Operational Research* 88: 203–214.

Surak, J.G. (1999). Quality in Commercial Food Process. *Quality progress, February*, 25–29.

Traill, B. (2008). *Working for the UK: Our contribution to the economy*. A report for the Food and Drink Federation, London.

Tucker, A.L., Edmondson, A.C., and Spear, S. (2002). When problem solving prevents organizational learning. *Journal of Organizational Change Management* 15 (2): 122–137.

Tuckman, B.W. and Jensen, M.A.C. (1977). Stages of small-group development revisited. *Group and Organization Studies* 2 (4): 419–427.

Unnevehr, L. (2017). Economic contribution of the food and beverage industry. Retrieved from the Unnevehr and the Conference Board website: https://www.ced.org/pdf/Economic_Contribution_of_the_Food_and_Beverage_Industry.pdf

Upton, D.M. and Kim, B. (1998). Alternative methods of learning and process improvement in manufacturing. *Journal of Operations Management* 16 (1): 1–20.

Vanderspiegel, M., Luning, P.A., Boer, W.J.D. et al. (2005). How to improve food quality management in the bakery sector. *NJAS - Wageningen Journal of Life Sciences* 53 (2): 131–150.

Varzakas, T.H. and Arvanitoyannis, I.S. (2007). Application of failure mode and effect analysis (FMEA), cause and effect analysis, and Pareto diagram in conjunction with HACCP to a corn curl manufacturing plant. *Critical Reviews in Food Science and Nutrition* 47: 363–387.

Wallace, C.A., Holyoak, L., Powell, S.C., and Dykes, F.C. (2012). Re-thinking the HACCP team: an investigation into HACCP team knowledge and decision-making for successful HACCP development. *Food Research International* 47 (2): 236–245.

Weiner, B.J. (2009). A theory of organizational readiness for change. *Implementation Science* 4 (1): 67.

Western Electric Company (1956). Statistical Quality Control Handbook. *Western Electric Company*, Indianapolis, IN.

Woodall, W.H. (2000). Controversies and contradictions in statistical process control. *Journal of Quality Technology* 32 (4): 341–350.

Woodall, W.H. and Adams, B.M. (1993). The statistical design of CUSUM charts. *Quality Engineering* 5 (4): 559–570.

Woodall, W. and Spitzner, D. (2004). Using control charts to monitor process and product quality profiles. *Journal of Quality* 36 (3): 309–320.

Wortham, A.W. and Ringer, L.J. (1971). Control via exponential smoothing. *Transportation and Logistic Review* 7: 33–39.

Xie, M. and Goh, T. (1999). Statistical techniques for quality. *The TQM Magazine* 11: 238–242.

Zokaei, A.K. and Simons, D.W. (2006). Value chain analysis in consumer focus improvement: a case study of the UK red meat industry. *The International Journal of Logistics Management* 17 (2): 141–162.

Index

Statistical Process Control for the Food Industry: A Guide for Practitioners and Managers, First Edition.
Sarina Abdul Halim Lim and Jiju Antony.
© 2019 John Wiley & Sons Ltd. Published 2019 by John Wiley & Sons Ltd.